She Left the Party Early

Minneapolis

FIRST EDITION MAY 2023

She Left the Party Early. Copyright © 2023 by Daniel Hauser. All rights reserved.

No part of this book may be used or reproduced in any manner whatsoever without written permission except in the case of brief quotations used in critical articles and reviews.

For information, write to Calumet Editions, 6800 France Avenue south, Edina MN 55435.

10 9 8 7 6 5 4 3 2 1

ISBN: 978-1-960250-83-4

Cover and interior design: Gary Lindberg

She Left the Party Early

Daniel Hauser

Minneapolis

Whoever survives a test, whatever it may be, must tell the story. That is his duty.

—Elie Wiesel

Also by Daniel Hauser

The Graveyard Gang (Calumet Editions)
Clodhopper (independently published)
Picasso's Errand (iUniverse)

Prologue

We have a lot of euphemisms for death. Some people kick the bucket or the can. Some slip away. Or push up daisies. Others transition over to the next dimension. Some are called home by God. Some simply pass. Pass? Pass what? Gas? Up until a couple of years ago, I preferred to use the most direct term possible: He/she died. 'Nuff said. Nicely cut and dried. But then my wife—the love of my life, the wind beneath my wings, the link that completed my chain, all that was good in my world—died, and suddenly the word "dead" seemed so clinical… so impersonal. Saying that my wife had *died* seemed cold, so I coined another euphemism. Is it better than the other ones? No, but it fits Whitney well: She left the party early. That's it. That's my euphemism. She was having a great time, enjoying the scene, the vibe, and then was called away. That's exactly what happened. It was a fantastic party. Everyone was having a blast. And then she had to leave, and the party was a party no more.

Writing this book has been damn difficult for many reasons. First of all, writing anything is a Herculean task. It's a chore that I, like many writers, will do just about anything else to avoid—*anything*. Things I don't enjoy—the dishes, ironing, folding clothes, going in for a root canal. Second, I'm easily distracted. Isn't there a game on tonight? I haven't played my guitar in a few days. I should water the plants. What's that, Daisy? You need to go outside? Third, the tapping of my muse is hard. My children will tell you I don't have the best memory. I forget a lot of stuff because it's inane, trivial, stupid or obsequious. I remember important things like birthdays, first dates or names of coworkers' pets (but not always their children), so remembering the minutiae of my wife's illness and death is a heavy lift.

A friend of mine, whose wife died of cancer a few months after Whitney, wrote everything down. Everything. Despite not being a writer, a detective or a court reporter, he recorded it all on paper. Why didn't I? After all, I'm a writer. I get paid for this stuff. I should have been journaling, capturing this life-changing epic on my laptop. Okay, I did write some stuff down, like when we were stuck in waiting rooms waiting to see a nurse so they could take some more blood. But I didn't make writing a priority.

Instead, I focused my energy on being in the moment for my wife. I wanted to be present—to make it clear that I was focused on helping her battle this demon. Deep down, I suspected our days together were numbered, but I wanted to put a brave face on it, telling everyone who would listen that we were going to beat it. The cynic in me had other thoughts. That cold-hearted bastard knows that life is not some Hallmark Channel Christmas movie. Sure, on occasion, people get lucky and stave off the inevitable for a month or a year or even a decade, but that's the exception. Cancer bites the head off exception. The "c" word is one of the scariest in the English language. Once it is uttered in a doctor's office, it can't be unheard—it is in your brain 24/7. So from that first diagnosis, I focused on being as strong as I could possibly be for Whitney.

She did the same. She kept her sense of humor, naming the tumors after some of history and literature's most famous serial killers—Hannibal, Dahmer, Buffalo Bill and Ted Bundy. Whitney loved a good downward spiral, and every serial killer had one of those as their backstory. I knew she was scared (how could you not be), but she fought like hell to hide it. She assured her daughter Sam that everything would work out. She put on a brave face when talking with friends and family, and she only admitted to being frightened a few times. I would hold her, tell her that I loved her, and then would crawl into a hole deep inside myself... one guarded by barbed wire, rabid dogs and something akin to the Great Wall of China. We would then let the silence envelop us in our cocoon of ignorance.

Because I didn't write a lot of stuff down, for the past two years, I've been returning to the scene of the crime like a detective trying to piece the story together. Reliving the horror. Doctors, nurses, family, friends... All have had to endure my questions that I probably should have asked at the time. At some point a friend of mine asked whether Whitney'd had HER2-positive breast cancer. "What the fuck do I know?" I snapped. I knew enough to know it was serious but not enough to pretend I was an oncologist. He looked at me like I was a dumbass and then quickly changed the subject. After all, my wife had just died. (For the record, she had HER2-negative.)

I keep telling myself (and my therapist) that reliving the past to capture this in writing is therapeutic. And it is helping me to process the pain to some extent, but it is kicking my ass the entire way. You can't hide from grief.

You can run away from it for a while—try to drink, gamble or fuck it away, but it will find you. I have found it helpful to do something that many guys I know refuse to do—talk. To strangers. About feelings. At length. Talk to others who have gone through this or are going through this. Talk. Talk. Talk. Cry. Cry. Cry. Emote. Emote. Emote. Help others who are new to the club—the club no one wants to be a member of. Share what you've learned or just listen. If you try to tough it out and ride it like a bucking bronco, you're going to land on your ass. Be forewarned—this is a solo journey. You can (and should) find others to help you, but it's always just you. You walk this path alone regardless of how many friends you have, even if you join a grief group of others who have lost a spouse. You'll be surrounded by people on similar journeys, but you'll still be alone. Some view history as fluid. Five years ago was yesterday. Tomorrow is a decade away. Some prefer present tense over past when it comes to remembering their loved one. Who's to say what's right and what's wrong?

In my monthly grief group, we'd start each session by telling our loved one's story—their name, the circumstances around their passing and the date when they left the party. During one meeting, I began with, "My wife's name was Whitney." Because it was over Zoom and subtlety is often lost in the virtual world, I sensed that some of my fellow grief groupers took exception to my use of the word "was." To me, it made perfect sense—Whitney was no longer alive. She was not going to come walking into the room. She was not going to call my phone. She was not going to text me. Like I do every session, I repeated that she was diagnosed with breast cancer in August of 2019, and 165 days later, she was dead. The rest of the group solemnly listened and then repeated their stories. One young man whom I'll call Arthur began his story: "My wife's name was—" and then caught himself. "My wife's name is…" After Arthur finished, a couple more grievers also used the present tense to describe their departed spouse. I sat there stewing, feeling like a schmuck. What the hell? Did the group see me as a hardened asshole who didn't think of his wife in the present tense anymore, like I loved her less than they loved their partners? I knew Arthur and the others meant no harm. They just choose to think of their spouse as a spirit, a presence that still exists.

Everybody grieves differently. Whitney lives in my head and always will, but she's gone. I'm not the kind of person who can sugarcoat it and act as if she still exists. A memory is not a person.

Along with using the past tense, I transitioned from saying "we." We are not a "we" anymore. We are an "I" now. When people ask me where I live, I now say, "I live in Minneapolis," as opposed to we live there. I have three kids; it's no longer we have three kids. I love that restaurant, not we love that restaurant. Using the royal we has been repeated so many times it becomes muscle memory and takes some time before you exorcise it out of your lexicon. I still catch myself saying "we" more than two years later.

While I'm adjusting, I need to get used to my new brand. For twelve years, I was Whitney's husband, half of Dan and Whitney, the married guy. Now I'm the widower, a tragic figure whose situation in life causes people to walk on eggshells, afraid to disturb my fragile disposition. Now every morning, I take the hoodie of widow-dom off the hook on the back of the bedroom door and pull it on. It's now part of my wardrobe—my personal brand. Inescapable. Oh, that's Dan. His wife passed away. Isn't that sad? Sad and joyless, that's me.

Waiting for the Ceiling People

"So this is how it usually works," said Donna, the hospice nurse, in a voice ravaged by years of Marlboro Lights and cheap liquor. Her "blonde" straw-like hair looked as though a comb made of titanium would struggle to pass through. Her pink, white and green smock had two large pockets on the front, which I assumed held her cigs, a Bic lighter and perhaps a pint of Rumple Minze. It was January in Minnesota, after all.

I leaned forward in my folding chair to make sure I could hear what she said next. Being the first day at the hospice, I felt the need to be sponge-like. Nurse Donna and I sat in a brightly lit back room where the nurses took their breaks to eat lunch or simply take a load off after a long shift of caring for people in their last chapter. Donna had started the conversation off by saying she had seen all sorts of inexplicable goings-on in the years she had worked at the hospice. "Go on," I urged, already numb to just about everything. What could she say that would hurt me now? My wife of ten years and the love of my life had been wheeled into the hospice just hours before. Her doctors and family had determined that the battle had been lost. Now it was a matter of making sure she was as pain-free as possible until her last breath—whether that was tomorrow, next week or next month. At this moment, she slept fitfully in her private room overlooking a snow-covered courtyard lined with mature oak, maple and ash trees. A pretty view, even with bare trees, for an ugly situation.

"If I've seen it once, I've seen it a dozen times," Donna said before devolving into a coughing fit. She held up a finger while covering her mouth with her other hand to indicate that she had more to say. I waited patiently. I had nowhere else to go. After gaining her composure, she continued, "I don't know where you sit on the religion spectrum.... Did the administrator talk to you about that when she checked you in?"

I nodded, thinking of the thirty-something-year-old woman who went through the paperwork when we first arrived around eleven that morning. I note her age only because she was significantly younger than everyone else on the staff. Some of the nuns may have been younger than seventy, but I doubt it. Being raised Catholic, I was taught not to set my eyes upon them for too long, lest you burst into flame and go straight to hell, so it was difficult to gauge their ages. All I know is that they wore brown habits. "Yes, we went over all sorts of information when we arrived," I said. "She said our strength of faith didn't matter."

Donna nodded vigorously. "Good, it doesn't. Not at all. Don't matter to me, that's for sure. The sisters might not like it, but they won't say anything. They don't talk much—at least to me. Maybe they talk about nun stuff back in their rooms. I don't know. But anyway, everyone is welcome here whether you believe in Jesus, Buddha, Tom, Dick or Harry, it don't matter. At least when you get here it don't matter. But it's likely when you leave this place you'll have seen the light. Most do, and you seem like most people. Anyhoo, here's how it usually works. Your wife—wait, what's her name? Something with a 'w.'"

I slid my right hand off my lap and let it dangle at my side out of Donna's sight. It formed into a fist, digging fingernails into my palm. "Whitney," I told her as calmly as possible. "Her name is Whitney."

"Right, I knew it started with a 'w,'" she said with an exaggerated wink. I didn't respond. "So anyway, usually when they get near the end they'll start having conversations with people who aren't there. You'll be sitting bedside and they will be looking up at the ceiling. Saying something, real quiet like. And you're like, 'What are they saying? Who are they talking to?' Sometimes you'll hear them say 'Grandma' or 'Granny' or whatever pet name they have for them, or they might mention someone else who's already passed. Then they'll smile and a sense of calm washes over their face, and then," she snapped her fingers, "they'll pass. Just like that. Like you flipped off the light. And no, it doesn't get cold in the room like that Bruce Willis movie." She shook her head. "Hollywood. I mean sure, it's a good movie. But it ain't like that at all. They never get anything right."

I had been listening to her encounters with the afterlife with a healthy dose of skepticism, but I agreed with her 100 percent on this point. Hollywood was full of shit. If this were a movie, they would have thrown in the part in which doctors came up with a miracle drug that saved Whitney's life, or she'd wake up one morning, blink her eyes a few times and suddenly be cured. Hollywood would have saved her. Most definitely. She was good-looking, white and middle-class. All the right ingredients. But this wasn't Hollywood. Reality aimed to kill her. From the beginning, when she received her diagnosis, to this first day in hospice, it was a steady descent. Like each day was another step down a long staircase leading into a dark, dank basement. No ups, just downs. One crushing defeat after another.

By the way, dear reader, you've come to the wrong place if you're looking for a happy ending or moral victory. It's my hope that this book will help you if you are navigating a similar journey. It will reassure you that you are not alone in your grief. It may be the strongest tool in your fight against grief, the bully, knowing that you are not alone. Having someone to relate to is a mighty medicine for what lies ahead.

"Sometimes they wait," Donna continued. "You know, until the room is empty. They'll wait until their spouse or kids are out of the room, like they don't want to die in front of you. But most of the time, at least in my experience, they start talking to the ceiling, smile and then pass. It shook me the first few times I witnessed it. I mean, I've never been the churchgoing type. My parents dragged me along as a kid, but I never really paid attention. I kind of liked the singing, but that was about it. As soon as I was old enough to call my own shots, I spent my Sunday mornings elsewhere. Like sleeping or not sleeping, if you know what I mean. But now, looking back, maybe my parents were on to something. After a year or so in this place, you find religion, that's for sure."

I leaned back. I wanted to believe her. I truly, desperately wanted to believe her. Attending church every Sunday had been etched in stone on my family's schedule. It was how we were raised. I wanted to believe that an afterlife existed. It had to. Otherwise, I would never see Whitney again. I didn't want her current state to be the last that I would see of her—bald, gaunt, struggling for breath. I loved her with all my heart, but the woman back there in her room wasn't the person I had fallen in love with or had spent the past twelve years with. She was a hollow shell, more or less, unable to carry on a smart, witty conversation laced with the occasional "fuck" or "shit" and sharp with biting commentary. No, that version of my wife left after a week into her hospital stay, which preceded her transfer to hospice. About that time, she lost her ability to even go to the restroom alone. Nurses had to help her with everything. Asking her every day about her bowel movements because she was on so many opioids, which do a number on your gastrointestinal abilities. They constantly asked where her pain ranked on a scale of one to ten, which she hated to answer because it was all too humiliating and unbefitting to a normal, functioning adult.

I couldn't blame her for checking out. Who wouldn't when life became so joyless and burdensome? At the same time, I didn't want to acknowledge where this journey was headed. Throughout her entire five-month battle, I refused to think the battle was fruitless. She would beat this. We would beat this. I had read enough books and watched enough TV shows and movies in which the cancer patient survived. The cases in which they didn't (*Love Story* and *Terms of Endearment*) were pure fiction, not grounded in reality. Donna had said it herself, "Hollywood. They never get anything right."

"So you think there's an afterlife?" I asked Donna.

"Well, I think there is, but you need to decide for yourself." She launched into another coughing fit. I could tell by the look in her eye she craved that next cigarette more than an eight-year-old desired chocolate. I had seen that look in Whitney's eyes plenty of times before. When we first met, she went through a pack of Marlboros a day. She tried to hide it, but I could smell it on her breath. I'd be driving up to her townhome, which she shared with ten-year-old Sam, and she'd wave to me from the second-floor deck above her garage with her left hand while trying to hide a heater in her right. She'd then rush off to the bathroom before I entered the front door to gargle a shot of Listerine in a lame attempt to cleanse her breath. One peck on the lips, and it was confirmed. "Last cigarette?" I'd ask. She would blush, mutter something about a "bad day at the office," and then promise me, "It's my last one." Eventually, she did break the habit but continued to crave those little fuckers every waking moment of her life.

After my little chat with Donna, I made the short walk to Whitney's room, where I found her sleeping. I decided then and there that I was going to buy into the nurse's view on the afterlife. It gave me peace of mind. A few months earlier, I would have scoffed at the notion. Logical, high-functioning adults don't believe in an afterlife. Not enough proof. When you die, you die, and you only live on in people's memories. I was nothing if not logical. It had taken me years to wean myself off the mother's milk of my Catholic upbringing. But now, because I so desperately wanted to walk with my wife again and hold her hand, I accepted Donna's word as the gospel. Okay, almost. I did need a little bit of proof. A smidgen. If the ceiling people appeared, I would forever believe, and at least a slim sliver of grief would be lifted from my chest. I could carry on more easily, knowing that someday Whitney and I would be reunited.

For the next ten days, Sam and I took turns bedside holding Whitney's hand, telling her that we loved her and waiting for her to take her last breath. After the second or third day, communication became nearly impossible. That damn cancer had invaded her brain and couldn't stop eating it, like the zombies Whitney so much enjoyed watching on TV and in the movies. The cocktail of painkillers they gave her didn't help with cognition much, either. Maybe Whitney knew what we were saying. I would like to think so, but who knows? They say hearing is the last thing to go. By this time, her perception of the world could have been like watching TV after the network went off the air for the night when we were kids—nothing but black-and-white fuzz. I shared the conversation I had with Donna with Sam and told her what we might expect at "the end." She nodded and said she'd had a similar conversation with the gravelly-voiced nurse, which made me wonder whether Donna was an evangelist or just liked to hear her own voice. Regardless, Sam and I agreed that we would keep eyes peeled for the ceiling people.

Run Toward the Storm

David Kessler, a grief expert (boy, who would want that job?), likes to reference the American Bison (although he mistakenly calls it a buffalo) when he speaks with people like me wrestling with the loss of a loved one. He notes that when a big storm approaches on the Great Plains, the 2,000-pound beasts run toward it in order to take it head-on. That way, they shorten their exposure to the wind and the rain. On the other hand, cattle huddle together, wait it out and thus extend their suffering. This is a great metaphor for the approach to dealing with grief. It's a storm that comes into everyone's lives sooner or later. Are you going to knuckle down and endure, run away, or lean into it and get through it quicker? Quicker is probably not the right word. The only things that seem to happen quickly when you are on a grief journey are breakdowns. They pop up without warning and then pass as soon as they arrive, like summer squalls. Otherwise, your grief journey moves at a snail's pace. Days seem like weeks, nights even longer, especially when sleep is elusive. You study the cracks in the ceiling. You take inventory of the late-night sounds in your darkened home. You notice smells that you were too busy to realize back when you had a life.

I think Kessler's run-toward-the-storm approach is the correct strategy. It has helped me. We all have to learn to deal with loss, whether it's the dissolution of a long-term relationship, getting fired from a job or losing a loved one. I've gone through all of these, and each time I've tried to be bison-like. It's going to hurt. That's inescapable. You can't drink, smoke or fuck it away. When you sober up or awaken the next day in a strange bed, it's still going to be there, ready to squeeze your heart like a vice. My advice is to face it, embrace it and work through that shit.

My wife died on Saturday, January 25, 2020, 165 days after being diagnosed with breast cancer. It was one dreadful development after another. This was no rollercoaster ride, no sunshine one day, cloudy the next. It was a five-month gradual fade to black. August 12, 2019, started like any other Monday, a bit lethargic and melancholic because we had to work. I got up first at 5:30 a.m. to take our pit bull Daisy for a walk. It was important to get her some exercise early before the other dogs in the neighborhood were out. Daisy likes to think she's the only canine on the planet and takes great umbrage when she is proven wrong. Whitney got up at her usual time, around seven, quickly dressed and left without eating breakfast. She said goodbye while I did my morning stretching exercises/quasi-yoga routine in the basement, just as she had ever since we moved into our south Minneapolis home in 2016. She'd bend down to where I was kneeling or sitting cross-legged and give me a kiss, tell me that she loved me and then head out to walk the fifteen minutes to the train station at 38th and Hiawatha. It would have been a normal Monday, except this day she had a doctor's appointment.

I'll let Whitney take it from here. She broadcasted much of her cancer battle on CaringBridge, a non-profit website/app created in Minnesota in 1997 that allows people who are suffering from medical conditions to keep their family and friends up to date on developments in their fight against whatever ailment is fucking up their shit.

This entry is from August 23, 2019, ten days after the diagnosis:

> About a month ago, I found a lump in my left breast. No big deal, it's happened before! Except this time, the radiologist was like, "Um, no. Not a cyst." Well, shit. As soon as that happens, all medical hell breaks loose. Immediately, there was a biopsy. The next day, sure enough, it's cancer. The tumor's name is Hannibal and he's a big, active guy. I hate his stupid face and you should, too.
>
> The following day, further tests and connection with Virginia Piper Breast Center. Next, a meeting with the surgeon. Hold on—in the middle of that meeting, we found out there's a second tumor! Hannibal invited a friend (Buffalo Bill), and they're having a tumor party! JERKS!! Making matters worse, they invited some lymph nodes. DOUBLE JERKS!!
>
> Suddenly, surgery is temporarily off the table, so off we go to Minnesota Oncology. I'll have five months of chemo, then surgery, then radiation. I'll be beach-ready for summer 2020!

So, it's been a couple weeks of tests, tears and prep, as chemo starts on Tuesday next week. We've had to adjust our expectations a couple of times already, but we head into this mess filled with hope and grateful for the amazing support we've received so far!

P.S. Little bit of a content warning: If you know me, you know that fuck is one of my favorite words, and I don't limit myself to just the one curse word. Guess what? Cancer hasn't changed that and has in fact given me even more reasons to drop f-bombs. Honestly—I don't know how else to manage this cluster, other than with humor and lots of fucks. I guess what I'm saying is that cancer hasn't miraculously turned me into a kinder, gentler version of myself! Ha!

So that's a taste of Whitney. She packs a wallop of information into a brief entry. I'm going to provide some more detail nonetheless. Shortly after 3:00 p.m. on Tuesday, August 13, Whitney called my cell while I was meeting with a couple of young women trying to convince me to hire their agency to improve my association's social media presence. I answered because I knew Whit had been waiting for a call back from the doctor to hear about the lump we had hoped and expected to be benign. Unlike the other lumps she had experienced, though, this one hurt to the point where she flinched when I hugged her too hard. When we made love, she'd warn me to be careful when I was on top and to watch where I put my hands. That was unlike her. Whitney loved with all her heart. We said "I love you" to each other dozens of times a day. We weren't foolish enough to take what we had for granted. Whenever we parted, be it to run up to the grocery store for a gallon of milk or to head off to work for the day, the last thing we'd say was, "I love you." We often fell asleep holding hands.

Because she didn't seem to be overly concerned by the lump, I didn't worry. It was probably nothing, she told me several times. But it was something, one big, fucking scary something. I took the call and told her I was in a meeting. "Call me back," she said. I quickly ushered the saleswomen out of my office and prepared for a sobering phone call. I spent a few moments watching the cars, motorcycles, trucks and semis buzz by on Interstate 35W like wasps in the eaves of our garage. I hoped this mundane yet frenetic vehicular activity would steady my nerves and slow down my racing heart. It was one of those ideal August days in Minnesota—sunny, lower-than-normal humidity with a high in the lower eighties, where you can't help but walk around with a smile on your face. "Walk" isn't even a good enough word to describe it. You'd saunter, stroll, mosey… perhaps even perambulate. There were a few puffy clouds in the sky, but nothing really to hold back the sun's glorious rays. It's days like these when you really appreciate the North Star State. You knew the days were dwindling down, like the old song says, to a precious few. The Minnesota State Fair would be here in a few days, and then, just like that, a door would slam shut, and it would be cold and windy, a land of snow and ice for five months.

As I punched Whitney's number into my iPhone, my gut told me that life was about to profoundly change. My grandfather Louie used to tell us grandkids that good things happen to those who expect good things to happen, a new version of the power of positive thinking. I truly believe this and try to live my life that way. But there's also intuition, a sketchy son of a bitch, like you've already read the book and know what's happening next.

Whitney answered, and I could tell she had been crying but was doing her best to put on a brave front. For as long as I'd known her, she had never been much of a crier, so I assumed the news was bad. I don't recall what she said exactly, and what she said didn't really matter. There was only one word that stuck out: "cancer." It's not the most powerful word ever uttered—that word is love—but it's certainly in the top five words goddamned guaranteed to stop you in your tracks, especially the younger the person hearing it.

"Motherfucker," I must have said. If there was ever a good time to swear, it was now. So I did again. "Motherfucker." Then, like the flipping of a switch, I shifted into caretaker mode. "What happens next?"

"Tests. Lots and lots of tests," she said, or at least something like that. I didn't write these things down. Why would I? I expected a full and complete recovery. I had complete faith in science, medicine and the healthcare system. (Throughout this book, when I quote someone, it's not a direct quote but an approximation, which is difficult for me to accept as a trained journalist. But it will have to do, otherwise, this tragic tale would be without soul.) "We need to go in tomorrow and meet with the cancer care coordinator. She will explain what lies ahead."

A long pause. "How are you doing?"

She was silent for several beats, then, "Okay, I guess. About as good as you might expect given the fact that I've got fucking cancer."

"I'll be home in a bit," I said, already starting to gather papers to put in my briefcase, which I brought home every night but rarely opened. My Catholic guilt told me to be prepared to work at home, my Irish side told the guilt to piss off and take the night off.

"Don't you have some kind of work thing tonight?" She had remembered correctly. A coworker had just put in his notice, and a group of us had planned to bid him a fond farewell at a pub. After drinks, I had also planned to pick up a couple of new suits that had just been tailored. I had joked with the salesman when I was first fitted that I needed to update my wardrobe because "I'm getting older. You know, going to more funerals and stuff." The salesman didn't laugh.

"Yeah, I'm supposed to go to Sean's thing, but it's not important," I told her.

"Go on. This is just beginning, Dan," she said. "We can't just shut down. We have to go on with our lives." She was right. We didn't know much at that time. This might just be a blip. Chemo might do its job and zap the cancer into pieces, and we'd live well into our eighties, seeing the world, enjoying our family, becoming grandparents and, maybe, great-grandparents. "Okay. I'll just put in an appearance, pick up the suits and be home by seven. I love you."

She paused before responding, and in that pause, you could fill an entire book. She eventually said, "I love you." But it was different this time. Not like the nine million times before. This time I heard it as, "I'm sorry I fucked our beautiful life up. It's all my fault. My body has let us down again. The migraines. The asthma. The anaphylactic shock. The trips to the emergency room. And now, fucking cancer. I wouldn't blame you if you just gave up on me. I'm like a booby prize of a wife. You deserve better."

All true, but not true. In for a penny, in for a pound, I say. Sure, she'd had some health complications. They were all scary as hell but manageable and surmountable. These ailments made her stronger, made her tolerant of others' failings, made her nurturing and kind-hearted. Made her the woman I loved madly.

Later she told me she wallowed, and deservedly so. Anyone who received such devastating, challenging news deserved it. She went to the neighborhood McDonald's drive-thru and picked up a quarter-pounder with cheese and fries, then returned home to consume a few old-fashioneds, her favorite drink.

I headed to the bar, driving in a daze, trying to process the news and anticipating what lay ahead. Telling the kids, siblings, coworkers, friends and neighbors. Nothing would be normal anymore. A book I had enjoyed reading immensely, *The Life You Dreamed Of*, had ended. I would be forced to pick up another, one I had no intention of ever reading. *Living (and Dying) With Cancer*.

I don't recall much from my time at the bar. Sean's wife and their two preteen girls came by, as they lived in the neighborhood and were comfortable at the bar. They planned to have dinner and celebrate Dad getting a new job. A few people showed up from work, and we had a couple of beers, but honestly, I don't remember much. I was on autopilot, asking Sean about the new job, asking his wife what she thought, but I didn't retain any of their answers. My mind was on a repeating loop—*Whitney has breast cancer. HER-2 negative breast cancer. My wife has cancer. The love of my life has cancer. Life will never be the same. Ever.* I couldn't believe it. What the hell? Why does this shit happen to good people? We volunteered. We gave generously to charity. We donated regularly to Goodwill.

I shoveled other people's sidewalks after big snows. Why didn't God pick some deserving asshole instead? I know I always preached to the kids that life isn't fair, but what the actual fuck?

Cancer's certainly not new to me. My mom's mom had breast cancer in the early 80s. She had a mastectomy and reconstruction surgery and lived another twenty years. My mom's dad (Grandpa Louie—you know, the one who taught us that good things happen to those who expect good things to happen) had it back in 1985 when I was still in college. He was diagnosed with lung cancer, which later metastasized to his hip. I remember Mom flying out to California to get his affairs in order and then making the tough decision to bring him "home" to Davenport so she could take care of him while continuing her roles as mother, wife and executive secretary at First Federal Savings and Loan.

I remember the warm summer evening when my brothers and I went to the Quad City International Airport to help assist Grandpa Louie off the plane. After the rest of the passengers deplaned, we walked down the jetway and entered the cabin. There he sat in first class, looking like a total stranger. Wrapped in a blanket, he was a shell of his former self. Leaning close to his ear, I said, "Hey, Grandpa," as cheerfully as I could muster. I'm not sure whether he recognized me; he just maintained a hundred-yard stare. For a moment, I wished I had never agreed to help—I didn't want to see him this way. I wanted to remember him the way he used to be, teaching me magic tricks (imparting on me one skill my siblings never had, which, being the youngest, meant a lot to me), taking us to Disneyland and SeaWorld and on fishing excursions near his home in Rancho Bernardo, California. Cancer robs us of our dignity. Just one of its many crimes. We got Grandpa Louie off the plane, took him home and set him up in my sister's room on the main floor adjacent to the bathroom. Mom had rented a hospital bed, completely out of place for a home that had always brimmed with life and vitality. The night after Grandpa's arrival from California, I volunteered to make spaghetti and garlic bread for my parents, Grandma and two of my siblings. Shortly after we finished the meal, Dad got up and walked into Grandpa's room to check on the patient. He returned stone-faced and announced that Grandpa Louie had passed.

A year later, my dad's mother, Tootsie, received her own cancer diagnosis. Lung cancer. She battled it for a year, going through radiation treatment, but that only made her weaker. The end seemed inevitable.

So cancer wasn't anything new to our family. It impacted the lives of three out of my four grandparents. Tootsie's husband might have gotten it too if he hadn't died of a massive coronary at age fifty-one.

While I had experienced what cancer could do to a grandparent, I had no clue about treating it. I understood the concept of chemotherapy and radiation but had never attended a session. Given how pervasive it has become, perhaps they should make a mandatory class on dealing with cancer in high school. By the time of adulthood I'd imagine that most Americans know, or have known, someone with cancer. According to the National Cancer Institute (NCI), approximately 39.5 percent of men and women will be diagnosed with cancer at some point during their lifetimes (based on 2015–2017 data). The NCI estimated that roughly 1.8 million people would be diagnosed with cancer in the United States in 2020. An estimated 276,480 of those people would be women diagnosed with breast cancer, which makes it the most common cancer diagnosis. Seeing these statistics defuses the "why me?" whine but doesn't make it more palatable. As Joe Jackson, a favorite artist of mine during my college days, likes to sing, "Everything, everything gives you cancer. There's no cure, there's no answer."

I guess Whitney was just going with the flow.

After picking up my suits, I went home, both anxious and afraid to see Whitney. How would our dynamic change? Of course, I would be supportive. I had always been whenever she had a migraine and needed to retreat to the bed to get through it. But now, instead of being part-time caretaker, it would be a full-time job. Would we laugh? Would there be silence? Would we be intimate or distant? It's a blur now, but I'm sure when I entered the house, Whitney put on her game face, and we embraced carefully, hugging longer than usual. We cried. We exchanged, "what the fucks?" And told each other that we would get through this together because that's how we faced every challenge. It probably took us extra long to fall asleep that night, but I'm sure we did it holding hands.

A Cabin Filled with Ghosts

"For fuck's sake, is this the longest car ride or what?" Whitney exclaimed as we hit the three-hour mark of our drive to the family cabin. She said this out of sympathy and a shared anguish because she knew that I had reached the point in the drive where I started going batty. And there were still two hours to go, past endless corn and soybean fields in southern Minnesota and northeast Iowa. We loved the cabin on tiny Leisure Lake just south of Dubuque, Iowa, but hated the commute. I had driven it so many times you'd think I could drive it with my eyes closed.

I turned down Bruce Springsteen's "Born to Run" or was it Green Day's "American Idiot?" We usually listened to one or the other or both during long road trips. It was Friday, August 9, 2019. The last normal weekend we'd spend together.

"I know, I know. I wish we had a cabin that was closer," I said, remembering how I had once suggested to my oldest brother, who also lived in the Twin Cities, that we do that very thing—buy a nearby cabin. It made perfect sense. We both lived in Minnesota. It would be a sound investment. Our lives would be so much better if we didn't have to drive five hours to get to a lakefront cottage surrounded by meth labs and people who liked to collect various automobiles that hadn't run since the Eisenhower administration.

"But we already have a cabin," he replied in a tone that told me, "Shut your stupid mouth. There's no need to belabor this point any further." I'd be wasting my breath if I ever made that suggestion again. Steve is nothing if not nostalgic, and don't get me wrong—the family cabin is certainly something to be nostalgic about—but it's five fucking hours away for people who choose to reside in the Twin Cities.

When my parents purchased the 500-square-foot log cabin in 1965, about the time I was taking my first steps, it sat a stone's throw from a tiny, man-made lake in the middle of nowhere. Now it's considered *almost* the middle of nowhere, as hundreds of eastern Iowans, western Illinoisans and southwest Wisconsinites travel there regularly to escape the pending apocalypse.

People from Minnesota, the land of more than 10,000 lakes and a half-million lake homes, always guffaw when I say that my family cabin is in Iowa. They usually ask, after they get done laughing, "There are lakes in Iowa?" Yes, folks, there are at least a couple of lakes in Iowa, including forty acres of the Y-shaped Leisure Lake and its seven miles of shoreline. The water is wet, the fish sometimes bite and the swimming, when the seaweed isn't too bad, is rather pleasant. When we were younger, there was even a beaver living on the western edge that would smack the water with its tail whenever you boated too close. In other words, a real, legitimate lake.

However, the lake wasn't always a lake. At some point in the middle of the century, a local landowner came upon a valley with a small creek running through it. Oaks, ashes, maples and pines surrounded the valley with a few limestone outcrops accentuating the hills. At the lowest part of the valley sat a small house and barn long ago abandoned. In 1957, the landowner convinced local authorities to put in a dam to hold back the water for the purpose of creating a lake. Once the lake filled out, he'd then sell lots and make all sorts of money. I'm not sure whether anyone became rich as a result of creating the lake, but somebody made a certain amount of money from my parents.

Dad, who was neither naturalist, he-man nor outdoorsy guy, came across a newspaper ad promoting lakefront property, and it quickly piqued his interest. I doubt that Dad ever fired a gun, paddled a canoe or wrestled a bear, but he and Mom wanted a place outside the city where, for a couple days a week during the warm-weather months, they could get away, sit on the porch under an oak tree that likely started growing around the time of the Civil War, and sip a gin and tonic or two. As kids, our roles were to fish, catch toads, chase fireflies, hike, explore, swim, build sandcastles and play Wiffle ball or Jarts—whatever, just so long as we stayed out of Mom and Dad's hair. And we did just that until we turned old enough to get jobs and discover the opposite sex. Then trips to the cabin became less frequent. As we grew older and had less free time, we realized how special the moments we did have up there. Living in Minneapolis didn't help improve the frequency once we had families of our own, but we made sure to get to the cabin at least once a year.

Pulling into the lot that Friday in August, we were ready to unwind. We had packed plenty of gin, whiskey, and beer and enough groceries to make all our meals for a couple days, so we didn't have to drive anywhere unless we wanted to. We had ventured down to the cabin a few months earlier that summer, but our weekend was beset by an abundance of rain and too many gnats. We spent much of the weekend stuck inside, going through the kitchen, throwing out old herbs and ten-year-old bags of rock-hard sugar that my mother had purchased long ago. She had passed away two summers before, and her children took turns going through all that she had accumulated since Dad died in 2009. Being a child of parents who had lived through the Depression, Mom held onto things too long. Whitney always got a chuckle seeing what Mom still had in her fridge in Davenport. "I swear she had jam in there from 1980," Whitney would say on the car trip back home.

"Really? That recent?" I'd offer.

Given all the "fun" we had cleaning out the kitchen during our first trip to the cabin that summer, Whitney wasn't exactly excited about another trip down in August. She had other thoughts consuming her mind, like the painful lump in her breast. We quickly unpacked the car, I made us drinks and then began cranking open every possible window, turning on every ceiling fan and knocking down a few dozen spiderwebs. Even though we shared the cabin with my four siblings and their families, without Mom around, there weren't occupants there every weekend. Spiderwebs were just part of the decor.

"Lot of memories here," I announced, taking a sip from my gin and tonic. Whitney had heard this a million times. She nodded and took my hand. It was impossible for me to walk into the cabin without stirring up some memory from childhood. Everywhere I turned, I saw Mom and Dad or my grandparents, who visited the cabin whenever they were in Iowa. I'd see my children as babies learning how to crawl or, in my daughter's case, bounce. She skipped crawling and progressed to bouncing across the room as an infant. There is video footage to prove these bombastic claims if anyone needs proof. The cabin was and continues to be magical.

The weather turned out to be ideal that weekend. Highs in the eighties, lows in the sixties with huge, Simpsons-like clouds and low humidity. Perfect for a roaring bonfire. We were lucky to have two during our weekend stay. After a couple of drinks on night two by the firepit, Whitney walked up to the cabin and returned with s'more fixings, which I knew was her top priority. I burned a few marshmallows and covered up my cooking hastiness with a Hershey bar and a square of graham cracker. If she was thinking about the lump in her breast at this moment, she didn't let on. We finished our sugary treats and held hands while admiring the stars embroidered across the sky.

Later that evening, as I climbed on top of her, she cried out in pain. "Aw, geez, I'm sorry," I said, feeling like a selfish putz.

"No, it's okay. You just… you have to watch out for the lump," she said matter-of-factly, shattering the mood.

I flopped back down on my side of the bed. "You keep on saying it's nothing, but it doesn't seem to be nothing."

"I don't know," she said, dejected. "I've had them before, and they always turned out to be nothing. I guess we'll find out in a few days. I'm sorry."

"Sorry? You don't have anything to be sorry about. I'm the clumsy one hurting you."

"Well, it's not like you're trying to."

"No, but I should be more careful." I reached out for her hand, and nothing else was said. I stared at the logs in the ceiling until sleep took me to a place where there were no lumps and life was filled with promise and longevity.

* * *

The drive back to Minneapolis, at least, that I remember, was uneventful. We spent most of the time listening to serial killer podcasts, one of Whitney's favorite hobbies. For as long as I'd known her, she had been a devout follower of books, TV shows, podcasts and whatever other type of media that delved into the lurid world of human predators. It was one of many ways she bonded with friends and our oldest daughter, Lily. When we weren't engaged in podcasts, I'm sure Whitney's mind lingered on what would take place the next day during her trip to the doctor's office. How could she not be concerned? Her woman's intuition must have been giving her warning signs. She had to feel vulnerable, wondering if perhaps this lump was unlike the ones before, that it was something sinister.

Day Two of the Rest of Our Lives

Early in the summer of 2019, a few months before Whitney was diagnosed, I started inexplicably lashing out in my dreams. Physically. As in swinging at things that weren't there, flailing my fists into space, sometimes smacking the bedside table and at other times, coming precariously close to smacking Whitney.

"What the hell are you doing?" Whitney cried out one night, waking me.

Groggy, I sat up in bed and gathered my wits. "Oh, my God, babe," I said, stroking her head in a vain attempt to pacify her. "I'm sorry. I was having a bad dream. Something was attacking us."

"Well, you almost hit me."

I felt terrible. What the hell was I doing? I certainly didn't mean to hurt her, but something in my subconscious put me into fighting mode. I don't remember the dreams well, only that I needed to repel some hostile force. At first, I wondered if it was my job, but then concluded work wasn't any more stressful than usual. My health seemed to be okay for a fifty-five-year-old male. What was making me strike out in the middle of the night? Now, of course, I suspect that the enemy was the cancerous tumor growing in her left breast. In fact, I'm certain of it. Somehow, I knew it was coming. My subconscious mind could hear it growing or smell it like a cancer-detecting dog. I wanted to protect my wife. I knew that something evil approached. Something that would destroy us, and I was scared.

* * *

The morning after the diagnosis (August 14, 2019), we went through our normal pre-work routine as if nothing had happened the day before. As if there wasn't a foreign invader in Whitney's chest chomping away. As if the word "normal" or "routine" could ever be used by either of us again. Being mid-August, I was in the middle of planning our association's annual conference, one of the biggest events of the year. A significant amount of staff time went into planning the late-September event, which marked the culmination of all the advocacy work we had done on behalf of Minnesota's physicians. While I was extremely busy preparing for it, this would be the first conference in eight years that I would not attend.

A year earlier, Whitney and I had decided to take her mother to France on a tour. Shirley had been scheduled to go overseas with friends in 2018. She had purchased her airline ticket and made all the arrangements to be in Europe for ten days, then she took a wrong step while walking along the only cobblestone street in Minneapolis. She fell on her shoulder, smashing it, and had to cancel the trip just weeks before her flight. It completely devastated her, as she had been yearning to visit France all her life. Whitney and I talked about it and decided that since the kids were out of college, it was time we started traveling around the world. We'd take Shirley to Paris and tour northern France for ten days in September 2019. It just happened to be during the same time our association holds its annual conference. Well, you only live once, right? We could go to France with Shirley, or I could go to Duluth with my coworkers. The choice was easy, but I was still responsible for some of the prep work for the big event. I had speeches to write, press releases to draft and various other duties to perform.

Whitney's work also kept her challenged. As an HR director at a tech company that employed a lot of hoodie-, jeans-, T-shirt- and sneaker-wearing millennial programmers, there always seemed to be one issue after another that required her complete attention and a lot of forms to be filled out. Add a cancer diagnosis to the mix, and you can imagine concentrating on work proved difficult. How do you think about hiring and firing employees, writing performance improvement plans and determining health benefit plans when an unwanted guest has invaded your body? How could anyone function normally? I would have balled up in the fetal position and hid under the nearest conference table.

Later that day, Whitney and I met at the Virginia Piper Cancer Institute in south Minneapolis for a meeting with a "cancer care coordinator." The institute, founded in 1990, employs a bunch of extremely smart physicians and other healthcare workers whose sole mission is to cure cancer. According to its website, the institute is "one of a select group of twenty-two U.S.-accredited cancer programs, and the only in the Twin Cities, to receive the 2016 Outstanding Achievement Award by the Commission on Cancer of the American College of Surgeons. The award recognizes cancer programs that achieve excellence in compliance to the Commission on Cancer standards and provide the highest quality care to cancer patients." Sounded good to me. We were fortunate to live in a state and metropolitan area known worldwide for its superior healthcare. We were doubly fortunate to live less than fifteen minutes away from all this expertise.

Upon arrival at the cancer center, we were told it would be a few minutes and to make ourselves comfortable in the waiting area. Whitney filled out some forms, the first of countless forms she would fill out. Eager to be irritated with something, I wondered how long we would have to wait. It was midafternoon, and they were likely running behind, which is what I've grown accustomed to over the years. That's why I always try to schedule my doctor appointments first thing in the morning. Physicians have had fewer interactions with patients and, thus, fewer opportunities to fall behind schedule. I knew the longer we sat idly in the waiting room, leafing through three-year-old *People* and *Good Housekeeping* magazines from the mid-seventies, the more my id would work to pry open the panic room in my head. *Do not go there. Do not go there. Do not go there*, I told myself. *You need to be strong for Whitney. She's the one with the tumors, not you. Don't be a pussy.*

Fortunately, before my id unlocked the door, we were summoned by Megan, the cancer care coordinator, who stood there smiling, asking us to follow her. If Whitney was scared, she hid it well. She smiled back at Megan and greeted her with a pleasant "Good afternoon." I probably mumbled some kind of innocuous greeting, thinking, "Who the hell has reason to be chipper? This entire fucking building is oozing with tumors." I kept my fears locked down and followed them down the hall, which led to an office overlooking the parking lot where our car baked in the August heat. It was another beautifully sunny day, a day in which all you longed to do was be out in it, sucking up the sunshine and the warmth, which in a few short weeks would go AWOL for months. Across the street from the parking lot, young men in shorts and T-shirts kicked a soccer ball around Stewart Park.

We took a seat at a small round table. I scooched my chair close enough to Whitney's so that I could either hold her hand or rub her back. I wanted to envelop her, protect her and tell her that everything was going to be fine. And I wanted her to do the same for me, to promise me that she would kick cancer's ass and that in a few months, everything would return to normal, and we could continue our idyllic existence. Of course, I didn't know it at the time, but those days were over. I would transition into a new role, an important role—a role that I had dabbled in whenever she got a nasty migraine or suffered an allergic reaction. Full-time caregiver. My wants and needs would be placed on a high shelf out of reach, where they would remain. All my energy would go toward Whitney's care. She needed a life preserver, a crutch and a safety net.

Megan handed Whitney a book that detailed what to expect and then launched into a spiel about tumors, lymph nodes, chemotherapy, surgery, lumpectomies, mastectomies, reconstructive surgery and radiation. Like most people, I had heard of all these terms before because breast cancer awareness is everywhere. Get mammograms once a year after age forty-five. Do self-examinations once a month. Susan G. Komen. October. NFL players wearing pink cleats. These images were omnipresent, but I had always viewed them as being for other women, other families. Not my wife. The panic door began to open. The temperature in the room seemed to increase by the second, as if the air conditioning had suddenly conked out. Was it just me? *Keep it together, Hauser.*

"Are you warm?" I asked Whitney.

"You know me. I'm always cold."

"Are you getting hot?" Megan offered. "I can turn the thermostat down a bit."

"No, I'm fine," I lied. "Well, maybe some water would be good."

"Do you want to take a break?" she asked in a calming voice. "We can take a break. This can all be so overwhelming. For both of you."

"No, just some water, please," I said tersely, letting my macho side flex its muscles. Megan was dead-on, though. Why should I question her? She did this every damn day. She had probably seen every kind of reaction, and the worst were probably from men. We really are pussies when it comes to medical matters. If we menstruated, we'd never stop fainting or throwing up.

Megan stood, gave me a reassuring smile and left the room to retrieve Mr. Baby his wah-wah.

"Are you okay?" Whitney asked when we were alone.

Mr. Macho returned. "I'm fine. Don't worry about me. This is about you."

"This is about us," Whitney replied, squeezing my knee. "We are going through this together. I worry about you. This has got to be tough on you."

"It's okay, babe. I want to make sure you are as comfortable as possible, be your support system."

"I appreciate that, but you need support too."

Megan returned with a small paper cup full of water, which I gulped down quickly. Whether it was the cool liquid running down my throat or the loving words from Whitney, my temperature dropped, my heart rate slowed and I could concentrate again. The panic door had been shut tight. Megan spent the next several minutes telling us what we were dealing with and what to expect. She handed us a binder and several pamphlets, including one geared specifically for the husband. I laid it aside.

Eventually, we were joined by the surgeon, Dr. J, who would perform Whit's surgery. She showed Whitney illustrations of the breast, lymph nodes, etc., and talked about reconstructive surgery and the difference between a mastectomy and a lumpectomy. She had been through this so many times that her no-nonsense delivery exuded the confidence we needed. Unfortunately, that confidence was shattered midway through the consultation when test results arrived from an earlier appointment that day, revealing that the tumor in her left breast (which she had christened "Hannibal") had company. There was a second, smaller tumor close by, which Whitney later named Buffalo Bill. A little explanation is probably needed here. For as long as I knew Whitney, she had been fascinated by serial killers. Obviously, she's not alone; otherwise, how could you explain the popularity on Netflix of so many shows and documentaries on people like Ted Bundy, Jeffrey Dahmer, Richard "The Night Stalker" Ramirez, John Wayne Gacy, David "Son of Sam" Berkowitz, and Joseph James "The Golden State Killer" DeAngelo? Whitney spent many hours watching shows, reading books and listening to podcasts on these lunatics, explaining that it had something to do with her love of a downward spiral story, perhaps to remind her that her life was pretty damn good. Equating cancerous tumors with serial killers made perfect sense in a perverse way for her.

With the appearance of a second tumor, Dr. J called an audible. Surgery would have to wait. She told us that we'd start with five weeks of chemotherapy, then, hopefully, the tumors will have shrunk to the point that surgery would not have to be so invasive. Without enunciating it directly, Whitney's cancer prognosis had gone to Stage 4. It had metastasized. We left the consultation with Megan and Dr. J in a fog. This unexpected turn for the worse would be the norm for the next five months. For an optimist like Whitney, it was devastating, difficult news that was hard to spin positively. For me, a realist, I swallowed hard and said to myself, this is the hand we've been dealt. Both were shitty points of view.

We returned to our little 109-year-old home in south Minneapolis in foul moods. It was becoming the norm. A few weeks earlier, the house had put us in a bad place late one night. Around 2 a.m. in early June 2019, Whitney and I awoke in our second-floor bedroom to a large crash. To me, it sounded as if a glass shelf holding dozens of Hummel figurines had crashed to the hardwood floor. The only problem was that we didn't have any glass shelves and certainly no Hummel figurines. I bolted straight up in bed, exclaiming, "What the hell was that?" Whitney did the same, though her middle-of-the-night utterance likely contained a "fuck," "shit" or "goddamn" in it. Daisy, our ferocious pit bull fast asleep in her bed in the corner of the room, lifted her head briefly, then lowered it, communicating in her understated way that there was no midnight burglar breaking in. Groggily, I touched Whitney's leg and said, "I'll go investigate." My mind ticked off a list of possibilities. A branch blowing into a window. The cat knocking a plate off the kitchen counter because, well, cats like to do that sort of shit. A light fixture I had installed poorly coming loose from its moorings. I walked through the main floor, checking every room and found nothing. Although the crash sounded too loud to have originated in the basement, I checked there, too, just to be sure. Nothing. What the hell? It couldn't have been a dream because Whitney had heard it, too. I trudged up the stairs and decided that while I was awake, I'd relieve myself. I walked into the upstairs bathroom, just feet away from our bedroom, and discovered the source of the crash. Sandy rubble crunched beneath my bare feet. I flicked on the light and saw a 2-foot by 2-foot hole in the ceiling. The plaster, which had been sagging in recent weeks, finally gave out. The floor was covered in bits and pieces of sand, cement and paint chips. I sat down to take a piss and assessed the damage. This was a serious project, I thought. Beyond my skill set. Write about it, yes, fix it, hell no. I flushed the toilet, washed my hands, brushed off my feet and walked back into the bedroom. "Found it," I said as I crawled back into bed.

"What was it?" Whitney said, laying back down.

"Bathroom ceiling."

"Holy shit. That was loud."

"There's a pretty large chunk of the ceiling now on the floor."

"I guess we need to move up the bathroom reno, then."

"Yup. There's another section that looks close to collapsing, too. I'll talk to some contractors and get some bids."

We talked about renovating the bathroom as soon as we moved into the house in 2016. It needed a complete overhaul. The window was leaky. The linoleum floor looked as if it had been waxed with mud. The claw-foot bathtub was stained and tired. But because the bathroom still functioned, it had not become a top priority for the first three years in the house.

Exactly one month later, while taking a break inside from a ninety-degree day, we sat in the living room watching a movie. As soon as I heard the crash, I knew exactly what had caused it.

Whitney jumped. "What the fuck?"

"Another part of the bathroom ceiling," I said nonchalantly, like Mr. Know-it-All.

* * *

Just hours after meeting with Megan and Dr. J and learning of the additional tumor in her breast, Whitney and I sat down at our dining room table across from our contractor Mark to discuss updating the bathroom. The renovation project would be inconvenient—we'd have to go down to the basement to use the bathroom. This would be especially troublesome when Whitney started chemo and had to deal with its energy-sucking consequences. It also meant we'd have to traverse two flights of stairs if we ever had to go to the bathroom in the middle of the night. I'm over fifty, so that meant my legs would get a workout.

Over the next hour, we shared our vision of the project with Mark, or, more accurately, Whitney relayed what she wanted. Black-and-white hexagonal tile on the floors, subway tile on the walls, a pedestal sink, a toilet that hadn't been flushing since the Harding Administration and, the pièce de résistance, a refurbished claw-foot tub. Whitney took a bath just about every day we had lived in the house and, for years, had put up with the chipped, subpar condition of the tub. It was time for a change, and she couldn't wait. In three months, we'd have a brand new bathroom. Unfortunately, Hannibal and Buffalo Bill couldn't wait, either. They were determined to keep Whit from ever using her new claw-foot tub.

Spreading the Cancer News

It is not profound to point out that divorce is an ugly business. After all, more than half of all married couples go through it, so plenty of people have firsthand knowledge of the carnage. Add kids to the mix, and it becomes a dumpster fire. We live for love. We are creatures that naturally want to pair off. We want to believe that this union will last forever. And then it doesn't. When my first wife and I were married, and we heard about another couple breaking up, I'd say, "I'm glad that's not us. I can't even imagine what that must be like." And then it happened, and we became another statistic. For years, I denied the relationship had reached its end. I saw it going south at about the ten-year mark when our kids were seven and three, but the optimist in me kept saying it would get better, that my wife would fall back in love with me, and when that occurred, I'd fall back in love with her. Plus, I didn't want to ruin the kids' lives. Having grown up in a community in which very few people got divorced, it was such a foreign (and, I thought, shameful) occurrence. But the low points continued piling up, and finally, we had had enough.

We decided to tell the kids one Friday night in early winter. We ordered pizza as a way to soften the blow for the kids, who were now ten and six. We agreed that we'd talk to them together, emphasizing that no matter what, we would always be a family, just one that didn't live together. We agreed that I'd start, and then we'd take turns reassuring the kids that they had done nothing wrong, that we both loved them and always would and that we'd be civil about the split. We sat them down in the living room and began to unload the life-altering news. Peter sat there looking confused, eyes blinking, as if I was trying to explain quantum physics. Lily put on a brave face. She knew plenty of kids at school who had gotten this "talk" from their parents.

Now, seventeen years after that horrible night, it was time to break some more hearts. Whitney began spreading the news on the evening of Friday, August 16, 2019. "Hi, Bean," Whitney began, using the affectionate nickname she had given her daughter when she was a baby. Sam's father's family had produced nothing but boys for some time, so when she was born, Whitney was quite amazed. "I couldn't be more surprised if she was a monkey," she remarked, then added, "She's such a little bean." The nickname stuck. "Hi, Momma," Sam answered tentatively as if to say, "What's wrong?" Obviously, when you've known someone all your life, you don't need words to communicate.

Two years before, on a rainy afternoon in July, Whitney and I sat at our dining room table talking about our workdays over dinner when I heard my phone vibrating on the coffee table in the living room. My first thought was that it was probably someone from work or a friend checking in to see about our plans for the weekend, but then something told me to answer it. By the time I rose from the table and walked the ten feet to retrieve it, I had missed the call. It was my brother Mike, who usually preferred sending snarky texts about something the Democrats had botched recently. Because he called so rarely, I knew I needed to respond immediately. It may have rung once or twice before he answered. "Hey, Dan, it's about Mom." I immediately flopped down on the couch and steeled myself for the bad news. Whitney, seeing the look on my face, rushed to my side.

My eighty-seven-year-old mother had traveled to South America with her sister to visit Machu Picchu and the Galapagos Islands. Since Dad died in 2009, she had been cramming in one trip after another on a race to see as much of this great big, beautiful world as she could before her time ran out. Israel, China, Russia, Africa. Now South America. On this day, Mom and her younger sister Sandy had been snorkeling off the coast of the Galapagos Islands when her heart gave out. Just like that. In my biased point of view, she might have been the healthiest eighty-seven-year-old walking the planet. She started each day working out at the Davenport YMCA. We thought she'd outlive Betty White.

I thanked Mike for relaying the news, told him I'd be down to Davenport in the next day or two and ended the call. Whitney enveloped me in her arms as I broke down. I knew Mom wouldn't live forever, but her mother and her grandmother had both lived well into their nineties. I figured Mom would be around for five or ten more years. Whitney rubbed my back, told me that she was sorry and that she loved me. She couldn't mend my broken heart, but she could at least keep it from breaking completely.

Now, Whitney played the role of pacifier again as she relayed her cancer diagnosis to Sam, staying as chipper as possible. "We're going to beat this, Bean," she told her. "We've got the best doctors. We're lucky. They know what they're doing." When Whitney relayed this conversation to me, I marveled at the positive spin she put on the devastating news. That's not my style. I'm a trained journalist. I used to report news for a living. There was no room for interpretation, just the facts. As such, it wasn't always an entertaining or pleasant occupation. Many of the stories I wrote angered people because they didn't want the truth to see the light of day. I always felt duty-bound to avoid any sugar-coating. But when it comes to dealing with your loved ones, sometimes you just wrap a whole lot of cotton candy around a piece of shit.

"I was at a friend's in-laws' cabin the weekend my mom called about her diagnosis," Sam recalls. "I was pretty upset and wasn't ready to talk about it with that group, so I kept it to myself that weekend. I believe I called Julia [her girlfriend] a couple times to talk, but that was it until I got back home. I wasn't shocked for some reason, though, when I saw her call come in. It felt foreboding. I was scared, and I could sense that this was going to be a big change and that I would have to face some big feelings. The rest of the cabin weekend was kind of a blur, but I tried to let the news sink in without spiraling."

Next on the list of horrifically raw phone calls came her mother. Whitney waited until the following day to give herself time to recover from her conversation with Sam.

"It was early morning when the phone rang," Shirley recalls. "I remember thinking Whitney never calls this early. It was unsettling for a minute. She had a hard time getting the words out. She finally said, 'I don't know how to say this, so I'll just say it. I have breast cancer.' I was shocked. I never expected that. No one in our family had breast cancer. She was too young to have cancer. I tried to ask questions without being intrusive. I kept saying how sorry I was. I offered my help, feeling it was too soon but wanting to be supportive.

Whit tried to reassure me. I tried to respond positively. She said she was going to 'wallow' for the day, and I said she was entitled to a couple of weeks. After we hung up, I sat in shock. I couldn't wrap my head around the news. I cried several times that day. Life changed forever."

Later that morning, it was time for us to brighten Lily's day. My call went directly to voicemail. While we waited to hear back from her, we called Peter. Like the young man he is, he took it stoically. "I remember I was in Madison, ready to leave for Milwaukee, when I got the call," he remembers. "I was filled with excitement leading into the weekend and was on my way to visit my girlfriend at the time. I sometimes get an overwhelming rush of anxiety for these types of phone calls. I love talking to my dad but calls out of the blue can sometimes bring difficult news. Once I heard about Whitney's cancer, it was tough for me to comprehend."

Lily had been driving in the mountains of Colorado when she saw that I had called. Being early on a Saturday morning, she sensed that it wasn't good news, so she kept driving until she reached a place where she could safely pull over, return the call and give us her full attention. After hearing the news, she put on a brave front, like that night when I told her about the divorce, but unlike that night, the dam didn't hold. "I got out of the car, dropped to my knees and felt like someone had punched me and all the air left my lungs," she says. "It was devastating and shocking and something I couldn't have imagined. I remember having so many questions but knew there weren't answers, so I just felt numb." Like with Sam, we told Lily that we had excellent doctors on the case, and they had laid out a good plan to fight Hannibal and Buffalo Bill. We assured her that we were going to beat this.

With the calls completed, we sat at the dining room table, utterly exhausted, feeling as if a giant had picked us up and wrung out all the fluids from our bodies. We would become quite familiar with this feeling. Each subsequent tortuous "update" call to the children left us drained and defeated.

Now that the kids and Whitney's family were up to speed, we began to widen the circle. I sent an email to my siblings later that Saturday:

> After a wonderful, peaceful weekend at the cabin, Whitney and I returned home to a harsh reality. This past Tuesday, we learned that she has breast cancer. We don't know what stage it's at yet, but the surgeon has recommended she get into chemotherapy soon, possibly as early as next week. They want to zap her tumors (there are two, which she calls Hannibal and Buffalo Bill) for four months or so and then conduct the surgery.
>
> Whitney's mom and siblings know and we told the kids yesterday and today. We are slowly sharing it with friends and co-workers. As you might imagine, this is a punch to the gut. We are scared, confused and pissed off.
>
> The surgeon is confident the chemo will "melt" the tumors away. She reports that she (Whitney) has a common type of breast cancer that is survivable. But it's cancer…

After sending that heavy message, I turned my attention to getting prepared for something lighter. A night out. After several days of one heart-wrenching incident after another, we knew we needed to get out among people, be surrounded by distractions, get our minds off the shitstorm that had become our lives. Wallowing was warranted, but you can't let it become all-encompassing. We had the perfect diversion—a home game of our favorite sports team, Minnesota United FC, also known as the Loons. We had been season ticket holders since they first entered major league soccer in 2017. The team had just opened its beautiful new stadium in April of 2019, and we—okay, mostly me—loved attending games, chanting along with the other fans and generally forgetting about life for a couple hours. If you have never been to a soccer match (or "football," as it's more appropriately called around the world), you are missing a religious experience. Fans wave flags, banners and scarves. Smoke bombs create low-flying clouds as chants supporting the home team fill the air, accompanied by drums and horns. Unlike other American sports, most of the noise made during soccer games is human-made.

That night we grabbed a quick bite to eat at a neighborhood bar and grill and then headed over to the stadium. I spent the entire game glued to the action on the pitch while Whitney scrolled through Instagram and Facebook, occasionally looking up from her phone when the crowd roared or to take a sip from her vodka soda. The Loons scored in stoppage time in what turned out to be a very exciting 1-1 draw.

"Thanks for coming out tonight," I said as we drove home. "You're probably spent."

"I'm okay," she said, reaching over to hold my hand. "We should stop by the neighbor's party when we get home."

"You sure? If you're too tired, we can just go home."

"But they're expecting us. We need to at least make an appearance."

I don't know how tired she actually was, but I'm sure she was running on empty. However, Whitney liked a party, so...

Our neighbor was celebrating his sixty-fifth birthday. Party tents had been erected in their small backyard, and a band performed. Under normal circumstances, it would have been a great bash, but our minds were burdened with a great storm cloud over our heads. Although we knew most of the people there, we didn't get up from our table to mingle. We drank, wallowed and kept our horrid secret to ourselves. We had told the kids and our immediate family, and that was enough for now. We would take our time spreading the news around for the next few weeks. Sharing it wore us out, and it scares the shit out of people on so many levels. First, it reminds everyone of their mortality, and although we all know we are going to die someday, we hope that it's after a long, fulfilling life and that it occurs during sleep so there's no suffering.

Unfortunately, that's not cancer's style. Cancer is the honey badger of diseases—"it doesn't give a shit." Second, people don't really know how to react when you say that you or your loved one has cancer. Some people say stupid shit like, "You've got this," or, "If anyone can beat cancer, it's you," or, "God doesn't give us anything more than we can handle." That last one really burns my toast. I realize that when people utter this pablum, this nonsense, this treacle, they are well-intentioned and trying to convey that we are stronger than we think, but it's complete and utter bullshit. If God doesn't give us more than we can handle, then how do you explain suicide? Suicide is one very definitive—

and drastic—way someone says, "I've had enough. I can't handle this."

So don't say stuff like that the next time you run into an unfortunate soul diagnosed with cancer. Just say that you are thinking of or praying for them. People with cancer and their loved ones want to know that they have a lot of people on their side, not people who want to repeat crap they've read on some bumper sticker.

* * *

Three days after the soccer game and neighborhood party (Tuesday, Aug. 20, 2019), after I had informed my coworkers of the situation and after Whitney had made the decision to go onto short-term disability, knowing that she would need all her energy to battle Hannibal and Buffalo Bill, we headed to Minnesota Oncology for the first time. It'd be the first of many visits to this outpost of desperation, where all who are battling the Big C go to linger and pray that the oncologist's prescribed cocktail will do the trick.

Minnesota Oncology came into being in 1995 through a merger of several oncology groups in Minneapolis, St. Paul and the Twin Cities suburbs. Today, the organization employs more than seventy physicians, physician assistants and certified nurse practitioners. It has eleven clinics across the metro area, making it the largest independent oncology practice in the state.

Following what would become a regular early-morning routine, we checked into the second-floor lobby of the Minnesota Oncology building, which sat across the street from Abbott Northwestern Hospital. The receptionist asked Whitney to fill out a questionnaire on an iPad while I tried to caffeinate with the supplied coffee, thinking if the chemotherapy didn't kill you, the java would. Looking around the waiting room, I saw a dozen or so anxious men and women on similar journeys. Bald heads covered in scarves, wigs and caps, and looks of pain, fear and uncertainty on their faces. After completing the questionnaire, Whitney scrolled through her Facebook and Instagram feeds trying her best to act as if this was just an ordinary doctor's visit and not the entryway into the chilling world of chemotherapy. I reviewed and answered work emails the best I could. The wait was alternately interminable and not long enough. I wanted to escape the thick cloud of depression that permeated the waiting room, yet I did not want to enter the back room, where smiles and good news were rare commodities. Whitney's name was eventually called, and we followed a nurse who we christened "Gloomy" because that's the attitude she wore on her smock. I can certainly understand how working with cancer patients day in and day out would be as depressing as hell, but you knew what you were getting into when you accepted the job, right? Whitney tried several times to get her to laugh or smile by saying something goofy as the nurse drew blood, weighed her and took her blood pressure, but nothing got a rise out of this woman. She performed her role well but with an inhospitable stoicism. Given Nurse Gloomy's demeanor, we wondered what the oncologist would be like. Was a lack of empathy part of the brand, the experience at Minnesota Oncology? "Come for the care, stay for the 'who gives a shit?'" Would the doc be another zombie simply doing her job? The surgeon, Dr. J, had spoken highly of her, even noting that she enjoyed a good bourbon now and then, which gave Whitney hope. After recording Whit's vitals, Nurse Gloomy led us to an open exam room and told us the doctor would be in soon. While waiting, I held Whitney's hand with my left and started taking notes on my iPhone with my right. A defense mechanism. By chronicling the scary, awkward situation, I could deflect its intimidating enormity, its sheer Goliathness.

From the beginning of the cancer battle, I knew I would write about it. It's how I cope and attempt to demonstrate my worth. It dates back to second grade, when I began writing parodies of popular TV shows that my mother watched. Shows like *Cannon* and *Ironside*. After writing a couple stories, I shared them with my teacher, Mrs. N. She read them quickly, laughing along the way, and then went on and on about how clever they were and how I showed such a natural talent for creative writing. That's all it took, some strange lady's adoration and I was hooked on writing for life. Moms are supposed to support their children with great gusto, but when it comes from someone who doesn't have to gush, it means so much more. One of my old friends from Davenport, and I use the term "friend" loosely because many times over the fifty-plus years we've known each other, we have not always been very friendly, likes to spout off clichéd dictums about how you can't sing the blues until you've lived the blues, or you can't write about life until you've really lived it. Well, my wife getting cancer would certainly be found on an ironic list of "living life."

I called my iPhone notes about the cancer battle "The Long Slog," although the slog, as it turned out, wasn't long enough. Here's the first entry:

> Another day, another waiting room, another exam room, another nurse, another physician. It's a long slog and we're just getting started. I'm tired. I can't imagine what Whitney is going through. She

> seems to be handling it well, at least better than I would. I've always been a minor hypochondriac, fearing the worst whenever I don't feel 100 percent. So far, none of my imagined ailments have turned out to be anything. My dad had a list of them, which I suspect will come my way at some point. Diabetes. Hypertension. High cholesterol. And the biggie, Parkinson's. A lot of reasons to be wary of growing old, as if we have a choice. But the scariest prospect isn't an ailment at all, it's living without my wife.

After a relatively brief wait, we heard a soft knock on the door and in walked the diminutive Dr. T decked out in old-school Doc Martens, black jeans and what appeared to be a black concert T-shirt underneath her white coat. Was she a Black Sabbath fan? We liked her immediately, and with every snide remark she made, we liked her that much more. She offered the straight scoop without it being wrapped in any kind of fuzzy bullshit. She treated us as intelligent adults who knew they were in for the fight of their lives. And the occasional f-bomb she dropped just made her more of a kindred spirit for Whitney.

Dr. T began with a series of questions about Whitney's family history, among other things, and then got a good look at Hannibal and Buffalo Bill. I looked away. I had seen Whitney's body from just about every conceivable angle. Every square inch, but not like this. I had no desire to see the growth that had invaded her. An enemy small enough to fit into the palm of my hand. I could have squeezed and crushed it. I could have dropped it on the tile floor of the exam room and stomped on it. And yet this vulnerable, diminutive growth would prove mightier than my wife. (Months later, I would find dozens of selfies on Whitney's phone that she had taken of Hannibal in our bedroom mirror. I'm not sure if it was morbid curiosity or to catalog its progress.) I also looked away because I felt like the sore thumb in the room, the lone male, the one who couldn't relate. Aside from my colonoscopy, I had always dealt with physicians by myself. Now, I played the role of support animal and observer, and I felt out of place.

Dr. T mumbled to herself as she examined the invaders, but I couldn't comprehend her words. When she finished, she put a reassuring hand on Whitney's shoulder and repeated the treatment the care team had recommended. Chemotherapy with one drug cocktail for four weeks, then more chemotherapy with a different drug combination for a few more weeks. Then, if the drugs have done their job, it would be time for surgery. "You have a common type of cancer, so that's good," she assured Whitney, but her tone wasn't exactly cheerful. (Aside from skin cancer, breast cancer is the most common cause of death from cancer in females. It kills more than forty thousand women each year. Most of these deaths are from metastatic breast cancer.)

Dr. T then talked about the port they wanted to insert near Whitney's right clavicle. It included a silicone tube that would be attached to a vein, which would allow the healthcare team to deliver medications more easily and efficiently. These ports can stay in place for weeks, months or even years. With it, the nurses would not have to stick a needle in Whitney's arm every time to run an IV. Nonetheless, the whole idea of having easy access to her bloodstream so the poison had a less restricted path made us queasy. We were putting our complete trust in the healthcare team.

Three days later, Whitney went to Abbott and returned home a few hours later with a new appendage. Whitney wrote about it on her CaringBridge site:

Saturday, August 24, 2019

> The kids are here! Months ago, we had the fabulous idea to have them all come home for the State Fair… it happens to be this weekend. Lily came from Denver, Sam from Pittsburgh, and Pete from Madison. It's the BEST getting to hug them right now!
>
> Yesterday wasn't the day I'd planned, however. Instead, Sam and Gaga (my mom) sat at the hospital as I had a port "installed," and a fourth biopsy. The nurse had told me (in Chemo 101) that I'd be sedated for the surgery. So, it turns out my idea of sedation (floaty, dreamy, don't remember a thing) is NOT what went down. I got something along the lines of Valium, so was undeniably relaxed, but was literally awake for the whole thing. AWAKE, meaning I heard every damn comment, snap, scrape, and sploosh. ARE YOU KIDDING ME?!
>
> No thanks to me, both procedures went fine. And I'm truly grateful they made

them happen at the same time—there were some last-minute scrambles involved. And after implanting a device in my chest and neck, and taking a chunk of bone from my spine, they sent me home with the best pain drugs possible. Haha just kidding! THEY SENT ME HOME WITH NOTHING.

So, I get it, opioid addiction has done terrible damage to people, across the country—maybe even in your own circle, dear friend, and I'm so sorry for that horror. I'm sympathetic to doctors, who are reluctant to prescribe them like they used to, not wanting to continue to contribute to the problem. But WTF? Tylenol?! You can't tell me that a pharma industry that's given us Botox in our pits so we're no longer bothered by sweat, and Viagra for erections on demand just doesn't have the resources to come up with a viable option for relieving pain. That, friend, is utter bullshit.

Anyhoo, I called my oncologist and asked for more effective pain relief. And they prescribed it. Lesson: We have to advocate for ourselves. It will come as no surprise that I intend to do so, very loudly!

And with that, we're going to the fair today! It's the very best time of the year!!

Your Girlfriend's Hot

I removed my sunglasses and rubbed my eyes. I was sitting on a wooden bench in the sunshine of late June outside the main entrance of Lord Fletcher's, a bar/restaurant on the shores of Lake Minnetonka, a short drive west of Minneapolis. It's the kind of place where junior and his buddies take daddy's wooden boat to impress the girls or play sand volleyball all afternoon, quenching their thirst with endless bottles of Corona. Given the clientele, it seemed an odd place for our first date, but Whitney planned to meet some friends afterward, and they only lived a few minutes away. So we'd endure a little bit of douchebaggery and have a nice lunch outside.

We had been corresponding over the past few weeks via a dating app. She made the first move. Her opening salvo via email made me laugh (although I don't recall what she said exactly), and I was certainly attracted to her smile. I responded with something spectacularly witty, and despite my receding hairline, a relationship blossomed. After several emails and then a string of phone calls, we agreed to meet on a Saturday at noon. Luckily, it turned out to be a beautiful day—cloudless in the lower eighties. I looked down and saw my right leg bouncing up and down.

For crying out loud, I was way past the age to be nervous about a first date. I tightened my canvas belt and smoothed out my shirt. I had arrived a few minutes before noon, wanting to get there before she did. I wasn't sure why, but I felt it would be better to be sitting down as she walked up, if she did. You never know. It's not uncommon for people to get cold feet or to completely come to their senses and realize a guy like me is not worth the time. Both online and over the phone, she seemed too good to be true. Maybe she would blow off the whole date, or maybe in person she'd be hideous. Maybe she had a mole in the shape of an anvil on the tip of her nose, or perhaps she was a George W. Bush fan who found Dick Cheney sexy.

Minutes passed. She was late. Should I just leave? Avoid the embarrassment. Cut my losses. I had only invested about 180 minutes of time on the phone. Hell, I had wasted more time on a bad movie. My stupid brain tried to short-circuit my happiness by building her into some mythical creature. My imagination had sculpted her into a modern-day Venus de Milo. What could she possibly see in me? Middle-aged, balding, mildly ambitious, eyes too close together, skinny-legged, flat-footed, fumbling guitar player, not that great in the sack. Not a catch for anyone, especially a knockout like her.

I stared at my sandals, wondering why I had put them on. I looked like a dork. She'd be able to see my toes, and although I had clipped my nails as best I could, they were not worth displaying. A couple of them looked more like cashews than human appendages. Oh God, I realized—I'm hideous. My heart pounded. Run, you idiot, run!

"Dan?" I looked up to see her blonde hair outlined by the noon sun, halo-like. I nodded quickly. Yes, I'm Dan. The funny guy on the phone. Please don't run away. I'm not that hideous. You could learn to love me if you gave me enough time. I'd like to say that my jaw dropped, and my heart skipped a beat when I saw her for the first time in the flesh, but I don't really recall because I think I was in a temporary fugue state. I had built her up so much in my mind that I had braced myself to be let down when I saw her, but I wasn't.

She looked awesome in her khaki shorts, sandals (with beautifully painted toes, bright red) and a white T-shirt with a scoop neck, revealing just enough flesh to leave the rest to the imagination. She smiled, revealing her bright white teeth, looking as if she had never touched a cup of coffee in her life. She wore large tortoiseshell sunglasses and simple gold earrings but no other jewelry. My heart began to slow to its normal pace, and I slowly exhaled through my nose. Perfect. Wait. Almost perfect. On her right bicep, I spied a tattoo, a garland of red maple leaves. I looked away quickly, but then my eyes drifted back and obviously lingered a little too long.

"Like it?" she asked, laughing softly.

"Umm, that's my favorite. Tree. I mean. Maple," I stumbled, unable to contain my natural dorkiness. I fought off the urge to be truly honest and tell her that I thought tattoos were the calling card of the homicidal maniac, at least, that's what the main character in my first book had said. (She would later read this and challenge me: "Is this a deal breaker?" But by that time, it was too late. I was so in love with her, she could have covered herself completely in tattoos, and I wouldn't have objected.) I had grown up disliking tattoos because of something my dad, who had been in the Navy, once said, "I never could understand why you would do that to yourself. The human body is beautiful. Why ruin it?" Of course, the kind of tattoos he saw were displayed on the hairy arms and backs of sailors who thought anchors, mermaids, and skull and crossbones were high art. Dad might have thought differently if he had seen the beautiful Whitney and her maple leaves.

"So, is that a yes?" she pressed.

I grinned, stuck in a virtual corner. What I said next could alter the rest of my life. "I'd have to say it's probably my favorite tattoo of all time." Thinking that I had averted a crisis, I reached out suddenly with my right hand, awkwardly, feeling, for some reason, the urge to shake her hand as if we had just completed a business deal.

She laughed and extended her hand. "Nice to meet you face-to-face."

"Nice to meet you, too." Her hand was soft, slender and steady. A hand that I would eventually learn could deftly swirl a glass filled with an old-fashioned without spilling any and could also carve a turkey or change a tire. A hand I could get used to holding.

The hostess guided us to our table on the deck, my right hand hovering inches behind her lower back. How chivalrous should I be, I wondered. I had already learned through our phone conversations that she was a proud, strong woman who didn't need any man guiding her to a table for lunch. I pulled my hand away and dropped it to my side as we weaved in and around tables. We ended up sitting underneath a large Heineken umbrella just feet from the docks lined with boats of various sizes. A waitress shoved menus into our hands and scampered off. I sat there, taking her in, my heart soaring. She had lived up to my expectations. After many, many dates, I wondered, could this be the one?

When Whitney and I met in 2007, there were only a couple online dating services, much fewer than the proliferation that now exists. Believe it or not, most of these exist—FarmersOnly.com, WomenBehindBars.com, Amish-Online-Dating.com, and EquestrianCupid.com. Being in our early forties, we were far removed from the days when people met in bars or at a party after consuming a six-pack of Bud Light. All my friends were married with kids, so wingmen were few and far between. I figured the most efficient way for me to find my next mate was via the internet. Unfortunately, it didn't turn out to be efficient. I kissed a lot of frogs, including recently divorced frogs with fake boobs, which weirded me out. I couldn't quite wrap my head around the concept that the way to reestablish your life after a failed marriage was to build a foundation, as it were, on artifice. I'm a nerdish, middle-aged man from Iowa who married his flat-chested college sweetheart. What did I know about plastic surgery? Wasn't that a California thing?

My first encounter with an artificial appendage came on my third date with Tanya (these are all pseudonyms to protect the innocent), a recently divorced mother with a five-year-old girl. Tanya and I had enjoyed a beautiful night under the stars enjoying a few beers, some laughs and music by John Hiatt at the Minnesota Zoo amphitheater. The combination of the warm summer breeze, the alcohol and the fact that we were pressed together like sardines in the tightly packed music venue likely led to the heightened amorous nature of the date. She invited me back to her home in south Minneapolis, and I was more than happy to oblige. She led me to her bedroom, and we began making out in the dark (we were both in our forties, after all). Approaching second, I realized that the reason for her unnaturally pert, middle-aged breasts was not because of her exercise regimen but because she had paid a doctor handsomely to update her chassis. Even in the dim light of her room, she took note of the quizzical look on my face. "I got those after the divorce. Like 'em?" she purred. I murmured in the affirmative, for what else was I supposed to do, and tried my best to act naturally. They were like hand grenades that both fascinated and scared the shit out of me. The awkwardness of this silicone discovery didn't prevent me from sleeping with her nor continuing to date her (until she dumped me), but it did wizen me up. I was in a whole new world.

    Over the next eighteen months, I continued to search for love through the web. It proved to be more treacherous than anticipated. There was Veronica from Latvia, who became irritated after I had asked two or three ice-breaker questions during our first date. "What is with all the questions?" she scolded me in a thick Slavic accent. "That's how people get to know each other," I offered. "Well, not so many questions. Is like KGB! Talk about something else." By this time, I should have been asking myself some questions: "How desperate are you? What the hell are you doing here? Are you a glutton for punishment? Where is the exit?" There was Molly from Eau Claire, who showed up to our first date already drunk and insisted on seeing who could chug a pint of Guinness faster. She won. I excused myself to go to the men's room and never returned. There was Jane from Iowa City, who wouldn't stop talking about her ex-boyfriend and broke down sobbing when I asked how long they had been dating. "Three months," she replied, the tears cascading down her puffy, red cheeks. "I loved him so much." There was Tiffany from St. Cloud who revealed, five minutes after we sat down for a dinner of cheeseburgers and tots, that her twin seven-year-old sons were out in her car. "Oh, don't worry," she assured me. "They're used to it.

They've gotten pretty good at entertaining each other." And then there was Gretchen from Edina who asked if I had ever worked as a clown. "You mean like a circus clown? No, I hate clowns," I said. "Oh, that's too bad," she replied, "'cuz I really have a thing for them. You know, sexually."

Dating had obviously grown more complicated since I met my first wife in film class at the University of Iowa. Now it was an endless string of go-nowhere dates to the point that I began to doubt that I'd ever fall in love again. Were all the good ones taken? Was this the universe telling me that I shouldn't be so focused on physical beauty? On Match.com, I admit I only reached out to women who physically appealed to me, and what did it get me? With plenty of fodder for future stories and not much else. There was the occasional lay, which would have satisfied the younger me, but there was no substance. No joy. No connection.

Then I met Whitney.

Sitting across from her at Lord Fletcher's, I couldn't stop smiling. I must have looked like a raving lunatic. I don't recall the conversation, only that I must have been charming enough for her to want to see me again. I assume we talked about where we worked, the presidential campaign, our siblings, our kids' weird friends, our past relationships and where they soured. You know, first date kind of stuff. I can't say that it was love at first sight (there was that tattoo, after all), but there was certainly a mutual attraction. After lunch, we parted ways, she to spend the afternoon on a friend's boat, me to go watch my son play baseball. We talked the next day and the next and the next. With each new conversation, I grew more excited. We had so much in common and could talk freely about anything. She seemed truly interested in my writing and that I played the guitar.

The following weekend Whitney and I went on our second date at one of my favorite sushi restaurants in the suburbs. I picked her up at her townhome, which was a twenty-minute drive north of my humble rented house in Hopkins, and we drove back down south again around Lake Minnetonka to Excelsior, a touristy town on the south side of the lake. It was a lot of driving but a great opportunity to talk. She wore green khakis, navy canvas Toms and a short-sleeved, white embroidered top with a scoop neckline. Perfectly appropriate for a forty-two-year-old woman to wear when she's trying to leave a lasting impression on a second date—mission accomplished.

At dinner, we shared a couple of rolls, some nigiri (she got her favorite hotate, and I ordered unagi) and a bottle of wine. We were feeling pretty fine as we left the restaurant and decided to get a nightcap at Maynard's, a popular bar a few blocks away on Lake Minnetonka. It was within walking distance, but I was concerned that leaving my car in the sushi joint's parking lot too long might result in a ticket. I'm a rule follower, which might have turned off someone with a wild streak, which I thought might describe Whitney well. But she didn't seem to mind. As we buckled up, I thought about kissing her for the first time but held off. We drove three blocks and parked on Lake Street just west of the bar. Sounds of the boating life filled the warm night air. Canvas sails flapped in the breeze. Waves lapped against the riprap. Bells clanged in the distance. As soon as I turned off the ignition, I popped out of my seat and ran around the front of the car to open her door like a chivalrous dork. She smiled and snickered as I took her hand to help her out. When she was clear of the car, I leaned in and kissed her. Instead of recoiling, slapping my face or screaming for help, she leaned into the kiss. I was no longer falling. I was in love. Our souls intertwined. Two hearts beat as one. I took her hand, and as if walking on a cloud, we floated to Maynard's.

The deck was less crowded than usual, which surprised me for such a lovely summer night, and we easily found an empty table. We ordered drinks, and Whitney excused herself to visit the restroom. Alone, I looked out over the lake, hypnotized by the distant lights on the other shore. I thought of Gatsby, basking in the warm embrace of new love. I couldn't believe my fortune. Whitney turned out to be everything I had wished for. Eventually, I noticed, out of the corner of my eye, someone looking at me. I turned to my right to see a curly-, dark-haired young man, obviously drunk, with a shit-eating grin. I forced a smile and turned to look out at the lights across the lake. He continued leering in my direction. I turned again, ready to ask him what the hell his problem was and why I had to be part of it. His gin-soaked grin grew larger. "Your girlfriend's hot, dude." It was a partially true statement, I had to admit. Whitney was indeed quite attractive, but I couldn't say that a second date meant she was my girlfriend. Also, this guy was on the verge of either passing out or puking, so he wasn't exactly a credible witness. I nodded and waited for him to say something else eruditely. He continued with his Cheshire grin and simply gave me a thumbs-up. My heart leapt for joy. How fortunate am I? Some drunk fucker at the next table had given me his blessing. Surely this was a night to remember.

When Whit returned from the powder room, she found me chuckling to myself, refusing to look to my right again lest I punch the drunken turd in the throat. "What's so funny?" she asked, sitting down. I nodded to the next table over. "You seem to have attracted a fan."

She slyly observed the young man for long enough to make a clear assessment of his intoxication level. "Yeah," she laughed. "Lucky me. I have that effect on losers. The drunker they are, the more they're into me."

I laughed. "Well, I've only had a couple drinks, and I think you're adorable."

"The night is still young," she laughed. "The night is still young."

We're Going to the State Fair, Damnit!

Without question, Minnesota has the best state fair in the nation. Each year it attracts more than two million attendees over its twelve-day course, beginning in late August and running through Labor Day. The Texas State Fair attracts more overall attendees but also runs longer, so ours—pound for pound—is superior. Located in the St. Paul suburb of Falcon Heights, the current fairgrounds are spread across 322 glorious acres. It's home to the Skygliders, gondolas that carry fairgoers overhead; a "tunnel of love"-style ride immortalized by an F. Scott Fitzgerald short story; a water raft ride with real water, as in, it's wet and translucent for the most part; a haunted house with an extraordinarily high cheese factor; and the Space Tower, an attraction that provides riders a 300-foot-high view of the Twin Cities.

The fair's gastronomical and people-watching allure entices our kids to return home from the four corners of America each summer so that we can soak up all that makes the fair great—the smell of fresh urine in the swine barn; the spectacle of Ma and Pa both proudly sporting mullets and walking their five-year-old son Jedediah on a leash; the guilty pleasure of consuming Canada's best culinary export—poutine, a delicious concoction of fries, cheese curds and gravy; a bevy of mesh T-shirts revealing bodies that should never be seen in the light of day; and butter sculptures of young women who compete to be named Princess Kay of the Milky Way.

Whitney loved the fair so much, she had an app on her phone that counted the days until it opened. She'd be damned if she was going to allow a bout with cancer to keep her away, so eleven days after her diagnosis and only one day after having a port inserted just below her left clavicle, Whitney, me and our three children loaded into a Lyft and headed over to Falcon Heights in the midafternoon. The plan was to go slow and take plenty of breaks. As soon as we entered, we stopped for drinks and took a quick photo by a cut-out of Paul Bunyan and Babe the Blue Ox, quintessential Minnesota icons looking right at home at the state fair. Over the next four hours, we paced ourselves and made sure we didn't overtax her, including all of the food, which really was the highlight of the fair. Given her lack of appetite, I consumed a lot of leftovers that day. She would take a bite or two and then pause, at which point I would finish the rest of the corn dog, french fries or gyro.

Normally we'd spend close to an hour in the stuffy Fine Arts Building to view the large collection of Minnesota-created art, from sculptures to watercolors to oil paintings to macramé. This time Whitney only lasted a few minutes. A combination of the crowded aisles and breezeless interior overwhelmed her. She headed outside early to find a bench in the shade. For the first time in years, I perused the kitschy art by myself.

I give her credit for persevering because I knew she was exhausted and that after the first hour or two, each step must have been agonizing. But the kids had flown in for this, and she didn't want to disappoint. "Such a fun day at the fair yesterday—feeling very lucky that I was able to go, and with the whole fam this year," she wrote on CaringBridge. "So glad to have the kids home for this time... and not just for Big Fat Bacon. As much as this stinks, I couldn't feel more loved."

Whitney helped me rediscover and fall in love again with the fair. I used to take my kids when they were young, but as they got older and wanted to be more independent, the fair moved to the back burner. I stopped going for five or six years and then met Whit. We had been dating for three months when we decided to take Sam to the annual get-together. As a rambunctious ten-year-old, Sam dictated which parts of the fair we'd visit. Unfortunately, that meant a lot of time on the midway, with its suspect rides and games of "chance." Being a "good" boyfriend and wanting to please Sam, I kept my mouth shut and didn't complain about the fact that we were surrounded by siblings on dates and dozens of likely felons on the run. I even agreed to go on a few rides with Sam. It was obvious that I was infatuated with her mother.

Knowing that we didn't get our quotient of the fair, Whitney and I returned a few nights later without any children in tow to gorge on sweet and savory treats, drink beer and watch all that is odd in Minnesota walk by. This is how it went for the next couple of years: two trips to the fair—once with the kids in the daytime and once at night, adults only. A transformation of weirdness always descends upon the fairgrounds when the sun goes down.

Because we liked to consume adult beverages while we people-watched, we took the bus, which dropped us off right at the fair's gates. We parked in a ramp close to our home in suburban Minneapolis and rode the articulated bus elbow-to-elbow with dozens of other fairgoers. Whitney always bristled at riding the bus, but she endured it so that we could drink and not have to park with thousands of others in suburban St. Paul. She'd just grit her teeth for the thirty-minute bus ride across the metro. One year as we left the fair, climbed on board and took a seat in the back, she turned to me and said sternly, "Don't fall asleep." She was all too familiar with the fact that my family has a healthy dose of sloth in its DNA. We often fall asleep the second our heads hit the pillow, and if we tried, could likely fall asleep standing up. So what she asked of me was no small feat.

"I won't," I promised, stifling a yawn.

"I'm serious. You know I don't like riding the bus."

"I know. I know. I won't fall asleep, okay?"

She quickly scanned the men and women around us, all appearing to wear beer goggles or coming down from a sugar rush brought on by consuming an entire bucket of Sweet Martha's chocolate chip cookies. Any one of them could turn into a homicidal maniac in the blink of an eye.

"You better not," she warned.

The bus did a lap around the giant parking lot and then headed out onto the St. Paul streets. Within a half-mile of the fairgrounds, I began to nod off. I could sense her glaring at me, so I pinched myself to stay awake. But I was no match for the sandman. By the time the bus dropped us off in Plymouth, I had slept for a solid twenty minutes. I awoke to find an irritated wife giving me the stink eye. We drove home in silence from the parking ramp. I didn't sleep on the couch that night, but probably should have.

* * *

If you are not familiar with state fairs—particularly the Minnesota version—you may not be aware of the propensity of food vendors to put everything they can possibly think of on a stick. It likely started with a hot dog, then transitioned to a corn dog. Once these proved to be successful, food entrepreneurs decided to go wild and see what else could be skewered by a sharpened piece of timber. Over the years came bacon on a stick, gator on a stick, pizza on a stick, macaroni and cheese on a stick, deep-fat fried candy bars on a stick, and even a deep-fat fried stick of butter on a stick (credit to the Iowa State Fair for this last concoction). So it was only a matter of time before some adventurous foodie decided to try meatloaf on a stick. I'm sure the main challenge was figuring out the proper meatloaf mass-to-stick ratio.

Whitney liked meatloaf and wasn't known for shying away from new things, so at the end of one of our evening fair visits, she gave it a try. She took one bite, chewed it a bit, then grabbed her throat. The damn thing was trying to kill her! As she gasped for breath, I guided her to a nearby bench where we sat down. She pushed the meatloaf into my hand, which I tossed into a nearby garbage can, then rubbed her back while she tried to catch her breath.

"Should I get a doctor?" I asked, panicked, knowing that the first aid building was not far away. She rooted through her purse and pulled out her inhaler. Once, twice, three times, she pumped albuterol into her lungs. She held up a finger, motioning to me to hold on a minute. "I think it will pass," she managed to get out when not wheezing and struggling to breathe. I began to pace as she waited for the albuterol to do its thing. I was not unfamiliar with this scene—it wasn't the first, nor would it be the last time she battled anaphylaxis. On a couple of occasions, we ended up in the emergency room with Whit receiving a dose of epinephrine. I learned to appreciate emergency rooms for their ability to save Whitney's life but grew suspicious of emergency physicians, many of whom strike me as adrenaline junkies who thrive on trying to diagnose maladies with about 10 percent of the available information.

After several anxious minutes, more pacing and a few more hits from her inhaler, Whitney eventually began to breathe normally again. We climbed aboard the bus and headed home. I didn't fall asleep this time. I couldn't if I tried, as my heart rate stayed in triple digits the entire way. We had dodged a bullet and learned to be a little less adventurous with our eating. Despite the nightmarish end to this fair visit, we returned the next year—we just couldn't resist—but that time, Whit stowed an EpiPen in her purse, just in case.

Work Gets Weird

Whitney immediately went on short-term disability. She didn't try to kid herself that she might be able to work once she received the diagnosis. She knew without deliberation that her battle would take every ounce of energy and that she couldn't waste any of it dealing with work bullshit. As the human resources director at a software company, she spent plenty of time reprimanding youngsters for their various lapses in acceptable behavior. Like the guy who regularly relieved himself in the men's room. I'm not talking about taking a piss or dump, but rather, a guy who would release his sexual tension into a rolled-up ball of toilet paper. At work. In the middle of the day. Imagine having that conversation and seeing the guy react nonchalantly as if someone had accused him of leaving toothpaste residue in the sink.

I, on the other hand, needed the distraction and continued my usual work schedule, at least to start. The Monday after the diagnosis, after informing the kids and our family, I sent a note to my coworkers:

> In many ways, the people you work with are like family. We certainly spend a lot of time together. And, as with families,

sometimes you need to share bad news. We learned last week that my wife, Whitney, has breast cancer. We don't know what stage it's at yet, but the surgeon has recommended she get into chemotherapy soon, possibly as early as this week. As you might imagine, this is a punch to the gut. We are scared, confused and angry. I share this with you in hopes that you will keep us in your thoughts and prayers. Thanks.

The staff responded with great support, offers of prayers, blanket sympathy and offered to help in whatever way they could. People like to do that—offer help. I've done it myself. What are you supposed to say, after all, when you receive the news that someone has cancer or some other life-altering ailment? You want to be of use to people who are faced with great adversity, but what can you really offer? Thoughts and prayers are about the only tools at our disposal.

One of my coworkers, Evan, took it particularly hard. He and I had bonded over the years, given our similar taste in music and our love of cardigans and sweater vests. We often attended concerts together and sometimes, depending on the band, Whitney would join us. Evan grew to love her, as did most people whenever they got to know her. Because he was unmarried in his mid-forties, I thought Evan was gay at first, given his attention to sartorial detail. He never shied away from complimenting me on a new pair of shoes or noticing when a coworker got a new haircut. He also often said salacious things that made me blush. As I got to know him, I realized he used shock value to disarm people. He and Whitney connected on a variety of levels, including their shared love of cursing, their battles with migraines and their reluctance to suffer fools.

One of our concert adventures took us to central Wisconsin in November 2015. Evan regularly patrolled the websites of his favorite bands to see when they'd be touring. When he didn't see a Minneapolis stop on Jason Isbell's fall/winter tour, he called me over to his cubicle.

"What do you think about driving over to Eau Claire to see Jason? It's at the State, an old historic theater downtown."

This meant nothing to me. We had old theaters in the Twin Cities, too. "What night of the week?" I asked, always concerned about being out late on a school night.

"It's on Friday the 13th, of all things. Is that going to be too spooky for you?" he chided me, grinning.

"Ha. You're funny. No, it's not too spooky for me," I said, still a bit hesitant, doing calculations in my head. Eau Claire is eighty-five miles east of Minneapolis. If the opening act starts at 7:30 p.m. and Isbell gets on stage around 9:00, he'll play at least ninety minutes or probably two hours. Then we'll drive back, drop Evan off at his house in St. Paul and drive home to Plymouth. Shit, we'd get home at 1:00 in the morning. I'm fifty-one years old—that's like three hours past my bedtime!

"I betcha Whitney would love it. Road-trip. A little interstate adventure."

"Okay, I'll ask her," I grumbled. "I'm not saying yes or no at this point." Of course, she loved the idea. Without any kids in the house, we could take off at a moment's notice and gallivant across two states as long as we were home in time to let the dog out.

Neither Whitney nor I were superstitious, but that Friday the 13th had a weird edge to it. As we drove across eastern Minnesota and western Wisconsin, news flooded onto our phones about the ninety people who were killed in a terrorist attack at a concert in a Paris nightclub. The City of Lights was on the other side of the world, but given that we, too, were attending a rock show, it seemed weirdly close to us. Isbell mentioned the attack during his performance and shared his concern about where the world was headed when people weren't safe going out for an evening of music.

After the show, we climbed into our Rav4 and began the drive back home, talking all the way out of excitement over what we had just seen, but also to make sure that the driver—me—stayed fully alert. Evan tweeted about how much he liked Isbell's performance. By the time we reached the Minnesota-Wisconsin border and pulled over for gas, Isbell had re-tweeted it. Evan was on cloud nine. His musical idol had shared his words with his thousands of fans—a fitting end to a fun, adventurous-for-people-over-forty evening.

* * *

Evan tended to come into the office around 9:00 or 9:30 a.m. His lobbying work often kept him at the Capitol late into the night, so it made sense that he'd come in an hour or two after the rest of us started. Because my desk was situated at the front of the office, I could see everyone come and go, which proved to be distracting at times. The day I sent the email to the staff regarding Whitney, he came straight to my office, put down his leather bag and thrust his hands out wide. "Can I give you a hug?" he said, sounding on the verge of tears. When he was a teenager, Evan lost his mother to cancer, so I'm sure my email unleashed suppressed memories. I stood up slowly, knowing that this would be the first of many awkward hugs. Evan was my friend, and I appreciated his support and concern, and it's not like I'm opposed to hugs, but I hated being in this situation. A friend reaching out to console me simply drove home the reality that my wife had cancer, and goddamn cancer almost always gets its way.

I shuffled toward his awaiting arms, and we embraced.

"I'm so, so sorry, Dan," Evan said. I could hear the ache in his voice. Like his mother, Whitney had entered a world of regular doctor's visits, hospitals, chemotherapy and, quite possibly, an early death.

Evan had battled demons his entire life. I'm not sure how much his mother's death played a role, but I wouldn't be surprised if it set him down the dark path. He went off to school after her death and tried to drink away the hurt. After drinking himself stupid for several years, he sobered up and then shared his battle with anyone who would listen. It's a similar story to Isbell—perhaps one of the reasons Evan could relate so well to the musician.

"Do you mind if I ask a few questions?" he asked as we ended our embrace. I took a seat behind my desk, and he got comfortable in the same chair he always sat in during our frequent visits.

"Not at all. It's good to talk about it, to get it out there."

"How's Whitney doing?"

"Well, she's still processing it, as you might imagine," I said, picking up one of the half dozen stress toys that littered my office. This one happened to be a foam baseball. I squeezed it hard enough that it disappeared inside my fist. "We're both still processing it. It's just so, and I hate to use this word, but… surreal. I think it may be weeks before we come to grips with it."

"Or maybe never," he offered. "It's a lot to take in. Is she going to continue working for now?"

"Hell no. She's taking short-term leave," I said. "She worked a couple of days last week after the diagnosis and was a complete zombie. Things are going to start moving pretty fast soon so she's going to concentrate on getting better."

"Good."

"Shit, I can't imagine working after getting that kind of news. I know some people do but my God… I'd probably just curl up into a ball under a table."

He nodded. "What's next?"

"We see the oncologist tomorrow, and then she starts chemo next week."

"Wow," he said to himself.

"Yeah, they don't fuck around. Speed is of the essence. It's a big old goddamn dose of reality, isn't it?"

He shook his head. "Fuck. It just isn't fair." He looked up. "How are you doing?"

I paused for a bit, squeezing the ball again. "I'm hanging in there."

He paused, knowing that there was more to my statement. A precipitous silence.

"As I said in the email, I'm angry. This is complete fucking bullshit. We've got tons of bad people walking around perfectly healthy, and then we've got good people like Whitney getting sick. Makes no sense whatsoever." I put the stress toy down on the desk and blocked it with a pen so that it wouldn't roll off. "So I'm kind of pissed off at God right now."

"A lot of good that will do."

"Yeah, well, if I'm going to blame someone, it might as well be the father of all creation."

He let that lie there, then asked tentatively, "Scared?"

I breathed in and out of my nose. "Sure. I'm scared. But I feel like that's a luxury right now. I need to be strong for Whitney."

"Don't you think she's scared?"

"How could she not be? She's the one with the cancer. It's just that she wants to put a brave front on it for the kids, her family, me. It's all just so much," I said, picking up the foam baseball again and squeezing it as if trying to wring the life out of it.

He nodded his head and rose slowly from his chair. "I need to make some calls, but if you need anything or just want to talk or vent, let me know."

"Thanks, Evan. I appreciate it. And feel free to ask me anything. Whitney is your friend, too."

He considered that, pursed his lips, picked up his bag and left.

Drip, Drip, Drip Goes the Poison

Six to eight weeks of chemo. Six to eight weeks of denigrating fatigue. Six to eight weeks of hair gathering in clumps around the shower drain. Six to eight weeks of puking your guts out, whether you consume chili peppers or oatmeal. Six to eight weeks of utter weakness. Simply getting out of bed each morning is a Sisyphean task. The routine, we're told, will be: get into Minnesota Oncology every other Tuesday by 8:00 a.m., and if things go well with the chemo session, get home by noon. The rest of the day, Whitney will "recover" on the couch, and I'll go to my job and try to do a full day's work in half the time. Wednesday and Thursday will be the worst in terms of nausea. By Friday or Saturday, Whitney will begin to climb out of the chemically induced lethargy, and then by the second weekend, she'll almost feel normal to the point where we might be able to go out to dinner and enjoy some time away from home. Then, after three days of thinking, "Hey, I don't feel horrible anymore," it will be time for another round of poison.

Minnesota Oncology's chemo lab in south Minneapolis is on the second floor of a four-story building overlooking the Virginia Piper Cancer Institute parking lot and Stewart Park, which Google Maps describes as a "simple space with sports fields." It's an odd way to describe any inner-city park in a large metropolitan area. Where's the mention of drug transactions and sex trafficking? Google Maps doesn't provide a description for the chemo lab, but if it did, it might read: a "complex place" with twenty-four infusion docks and no privacy. Certainly nothing simple about it, that's for sure. Each dock has a vinyl chair with a leg support that pops up and a back that tilts. The chairs are heated and vibrate if you so choose. On either arm is a tray that can retract or fold out to hold your phone, a magazine and your water container (everyone is strongly encouraged to take plenty of fluids, as it helps with the drugs you'll consume). Next to each infusion chair sits a guest chair for your caretaker, although some people come alone. Finally, there's the infusion pump, the precise administer of the chemo meds, which is equipped with wheels so you can guide it into the bathroom if you need to relieve yourself during your multi-hour session.

We were greeted on our first visit by a short, matronly woman who looked to be in her early sixties. "Pick a spot, any spot," she said, sweeping her arm dramatically as if showing off the next showcase on *The Price is Right*. Having arrived early, we had our pick of the stations. Only a few other patients were getting their infusions. By the time we left a few hours later, though, nearly all the stations were in use. The hostess offered Whitney a warm blanket and made sure we knew how to control the closest flat-screen TV, one of several mounted around the room. Instead of TV, Whitney opted to listen to a serial killer podcast. Some patients like Whitney put on headphones and closed their eyes in a desperate attempt to steal away to some private place in their heads. Some fell asleep, obviously veterans of many chemo sessions. On one of our earlier visits, one patient snored for a good chunk of his session. Others watched MSNBC or Fox News, apparently because it helps to distract you from your chemo treatment by getting you irritated as fuck at the opposing political party. Still others roam the chemo lab, wheeling along with their infusion pump, greeting anyone who will acknowledge them. One chatty patient started or ended each of his lengthy one-sided conversations with reference to the Green Bay Packers, be it Aaron Rodgers' passing proficiency or the team's long history of winning.

"What the fuck? Why is there so much cancer?" I typed into the Notes app on my iPhone. "What is wrong with us? Are we devolving? I kind of think so. How else do you explain electing a former reality TV star as president? As a people, we are getting considerably dumber. And meaner. Maybe making cancer so prevalent is God's revenge. 'Look at all the riches I've given you, and you a) take them for granted and b) are doing your best to destroy them.' Whitney is paying for other people's greed, waste and general indecency."

After venting into my smartphone, I switched on my work laptop and tried to concentrate on anything but our location. I inserted my earbuds and listened to classical music in a futile attempt to remain calm. To my right, a nurse piloted a cannula into Whit's port and connected it to the infusion pump. I paused my music to listen as the nurse reviewed the possible side effects of the chemicals, while a voice in my head kept repeating, "This can't be happening, this can't be happening, this can't be happening." In the past two weeks, we had learned of the first tumor, the second, had several biopsies, a port placed in her upper chest and now chemotherapy. It all zoomed by at a terrifying pace.

With cancer, there is no lollygagging. You can't react to it gingerly. It's literally kill or be killed, and now it was time to kill the cancer with very strong chemicals like doxorubicin. As Dr. T explained to us, the chemo medications attack fast-growing cells in your body—and cancer is one speedy motherfucker.

As the infusion pump did its job, Whitney drifted off to her inner fortress, where she could deal with the monumental task of fighting Hannibal and Buffalo Bill. I pecked away at the computer, trying to concentrate on work. I wanted to scream. I wanted to run. I wanted to kick Hannibal and Buffalo Bill squarely in the nuts. A John Oliver-esque thrashing played in my head:

> Okay, listen up, you little shit, rat bastards, conglomerations of abnormality, you can fuck right off. Now! No one invited you. You're not wanted here. Get out of my wife, you pathetic fornicators! You think you've got a job to do. Well, if you do, it's a completely useless, shitty job. You want to grow, add cells to your mass and procreate so that you multiply like goddamn rabbits. But you're not rabbits, are you? Rabbits are cute. Rabbits are cuddly. Rabbits are downright adorable. You're fucking ugly, so ugly your mother doesn't even love you. She recoils at the sight of you. Is that why you're so angry because your mummy doesn't love you? You take your frustrations out on innocent people. You ruin their lives so that it makes you feel better about your

complete hideousness. Well, fuck off.
It's not going to end well for you. You're
goddamn barnacles attaching yourself
to the Titanic. If you are successful, you
are all going to die, and for what? You're
not fighting for democracy or family
(remember, your mummy hates you).
There's nothing noble about your cause.
You're not going to take over the world.
In the end, what will you achieve? You'll
become indistinguishable ash, and your
legacy is that of being complete assholes.
Just drink up that chemo and die, you
worthless pieces of shit.

About an hour into Whitney's session, I noticed the man across from us acting as if someone had just poured a petri dish full of fire ants down his BVDs. "Nurse, I'm feeling a bit nauseous and getting quite hot," he said, agitated. The nurse quickly grabbed a vial of Benadryl and connected it to his IV. In short order, the patient's nausea and spike in temperature abated and he drifted off to sleep. I couldn't believe how calmly the nurse treated the incident. I thought I was going to watch him die. That's where my mind was at. Great first impression of the chemo lab for Whit and me; neither of us wanted to come back. Unfortunately, we were just getting started.

Whitney's CaringBridge Entry, August 27, 2019

Wheeee!! First round of chemo done! No
problems and the staff at MN Oncology
made us so comfortable and cared for.

They give some long-lasting anti-nausea with the chemo, so I should be good for a couple days, even without taking any of the two nausea Rx's I have.

So, two things: When I tended bar in the early 90s, I made up a shot called the "Wild Thing." Like most all of my late-80s, early-90s memories, I'm somewhat foggy on the details. Might have been vodka, peach schnapps, Malibu rum, cranberry juice, and a splash of 7Up. Shake it with ice, strain, and toss it back. Anyhoo, it sure did have a moment, as we'd make them up by the pitcher! So, if you check out the pic attached to this post, know that I was pretending they were injecting Wild Things, rather than actual poison.

Second thing: Can confirm that pee turns red with this treatment! My nurse suggested the same may be true for tears. I'm planning a little pity party this afternoon and will tell you if it's true.

So grateful for those who've reached out to us with support and those who are quietly lurking here. We appreciate you so much!

We learned quickly that chemotherapy didn't fuck around. I left for work the next day (Wednesday) with

Whitney still in bed, and when I returned later, around five, she was sacked out on the couch. She made some joke about having a "super productive" day, and I reminded her that her job was to get better, and if that meant laying around all day, then so be it.

On Thursday, as she still battled overwhelming fatigue, the hospital called and gave her the results of the biopsy she got the same day they installed her port—the cancer had spread to her spine. This tumor, which she called "Ted Bundy, because he was a real asshole," meant she was now officially Stage Four. At this point, I think we would have been justified in giving up. Barely weeks into this battle and we were already finding that the cancer was not curable. There would be no Hollywood ending in our future. Whit's straight-talking oncologist tried to reassure us that advances in medicine happen all the time. Perhaps a breakthrough would happen for us. Perhaps some scientist in some lab somewhere in the world would discover a miracle drug in time to save Whitney. Or perhaps we were just screwed.

Alone in Louisville

Three days after her first chemo treatment and a day after learning that her cancer was incurable, we were scheduled to get on a plane and fly to Louisville, where my sister's middle child was getting married. Whitney had every intention of attending the celebration. Even the night before, just hours after hearing about the third tumor and struggling to stay upright to pack her bag, she thought she could do it. We had rented an Airbnb not far from my sister's home and planned to share it with Lily and Pete. More family time would be a great distraction from the hell we were going through, but that night Whitney slept maybe two hours. The next morning she struggled to get out of bed to go to the bathroom. Upon her return, she said, "I'm sorry, I just can't do it. I want to go to the wedding, but I feel like shit. I would be holding you back the entire time."

"No, you wouldn't," I said, but of course, she would. My sister had the entire weekend planned out, and it didn't include time to recover from chemo. Given Whit's fondness for bourbon, we had asked Mary to schedule a distillery tour, and of course, we'd work in a trip to Churchill Downs. Then there were the rehearsal dinner and the actual wedding. The entire three days in Louisville would be go, go, go. I wanted a healthy Whitney along, not this new version.

"Yes, I would. I can barely make it from the bedroom to the couch. Sam will be here. She can take care of me. We'll drink wine and watch chick flicks. It will almost be as good as going to Kentucky."

I kissed her forehead and guided her back down onto the bed. We were fortunate that Sam had planned to come back to Minneapolis to see her father just a week after being here for the fair. Lily had stayed in Minneapolis the entire week, while Peter had returned to Madison. He'd fly to Louisville later in the day to meet up with me and Lil. It was too late to change Whit's ticket as the flight was only three hours away, so I'd fly to Louisville next to an empty seat.

Lily and I drove to the airport together but were on separate flights. I sat at my gate alone, lost in my thoughts. Was this the beginning of my life alone? For the first fifty-five years of my life, I was rarely a solo act. Growing up in a small house and sharing a room with three brothers, you learned to be around people. I didn't get my own room until my sophomore year of college, then met my first wife and lived with her and then the kids for the next eighteen years. After the divorce, I had the kids half of the week, so I never really felt like I lived on my own. By the time the kids grew up and moved out, Whitney and I were married. Living alone for any length of time seemed like a foreign concept. Still is. Some people like it, choose it, revel in it. Not me. Maybe I'll get used to it someday, but for now, I want to have someone sitting across from me during meals. I don't want the entire couch to myself. I want someone who I can download the day's happenings and listen to me gripe when someone or something is pissing me off at work. And vice versa. I want to hear someone else's stories and troubles. It's part of being an adult.

As I contemplated being alone, the intercom system blasted out a variety of safety messages and announced that such-and-such flight had been overbooked. Then it dawned on me that the airline would be expecting Whitney to be on the plane. We hadn't done anything with the ticket. I didn't want to sit by a stranger, but who knows? Maybe there was a solo traveler trying to get back home to Louisville to visit his sick grandmother or see his children for the first time in months. I awkwardly approached the gate agent; it was all so weird to me that my wife had cancer and would not be on the plane.

"Good morning, may I help you?" the agent asked with a smile.

I paused, which is not like me. Usually, I jump in guns a-blazing whenever I communicate. After all, that's what I get paid to do. But how should I respond? Use this unsuspecting stranger as a conduit to vent? "Hi, Tonya. My wife won't be on the flight because she's sick from her reaction to chemotherapy? Yeah, she's got breast cancer, stage four, incurable, so consider yourself lucky! Whatever issues you have herding people onto planes pales in comparison to what she, and consequently, I must deal with. In fact, your life is probably a fucking walk in the park, isn't it, Tonya? Hmmm?" I did not unload on Tonya. It wasn't her fault. A few months after this interaction, Tonya would be lucky to even have a job, given the COVID-19 pandemic's devastating effect on the travel industry. Instead, I told her, calmly: "My wife will not be on the flight. She's sick and unable to travel."

"Oh, I'm sorry to hear that, Mr. Hauser."

"I just wanted to let you know so you don't go announcing her name on the intercom. You could probably release her seat if it's a full flight."

"It's not a full flight, so I guess you will have a little more room to stretch out." She smiled and turned back to her computer screen, signifying that I should go sit down, which I did obediently.

I pulled out my phone and started scrolling through Facebook and Instagram but decided I couldn't concentrate on anything, so I spent the remainder of my wait observing all the activity in the terminal. A young couple tended to their toddler, who had a hard time sitting still. A young mother read a small, colorful book to her son. An old couple had a brief discussion, then the wife pulled out a book of crossword puzzles, and the husband closed his eyes, intent on dozing off. Dozens of various travelers anxiously walked past on the way to their gate or toward baggage claim.

Thirty minutes later, I sat on the plane, the warm sunshine coming in through the window to my left and shining on the empty seat. I thought more about being alone during the weekend ahead. Everything about it would be awkward and weird. Nothing would be normal anymore. There'd always be a fog, an uneasiness. How will people react to me? Do they see me now as the guy whose wife has cancer? As the soon-to-be widower? People kept asking me how I was doing. I didn't know how to respond. The love of my life lives in constant pain. Every day is a slog. The oncologist told us that "people with stage four can live up to ten years." Ten fucking years! Are you kidding me? That's not enough!

I closed my eyes and tried to sleep during the two-hour flight, but instead, I spent the time wallowing and assessing my situation. I have lived a privileged life. That fact is not lost on me. I am male. I am white. I am straight. I am tall. I am slender. I grew up in an upper-middle-class family with parents who were married for more than fifty years. I have my health. I'm gainfully employed. I'm college educated. I have enough charm that I can make friends (or at least converse) with most people. I don't want for anything. We own a nice (be it small) house in a generally quiet neighborhood with wonderful, funny, talented, caring neighbors. I have never had to walk in another person's shoes. I can walk my dog each morning in the dark and never fear for my safety. I'm not worried about being pulled over by the police and being shot. The only personal features someone could mock is my bald head and perhaps my skinny legs. But now I'm confronted with my wife's mortality, and suddenly, I feel that I can put my grief up against anyone else's as if we are all graded on some kind of misery index. Oh, you've been discriminated against your entire life because you're Black? Well, my wife has cancer. You've had to fend off the unwelcome advances of just about every male you've ever worked with because you're an attractive female? Did I tell you my wife has cancer? What about you? You have no autoimmune defenses, so you must live inside a bubble? But you don't have cancer, right?

Self-pity can be stifling.

Later that night in Louisville, after we had enjoyed dinner and drinks at my sister's house with the rest of my family, Lily, Peter and I returned to our rented house a few miles away. I retired to the second-floor bedroom where Whitney and I were to sleep. I closed the door and lay down exhausted. Instead of sleeping in the middle of the queen bed, I chose to sleep on the left side. Whitney always had me sleep closest to the door in case some homicidal maniac entered in the middle of the night. That way, he'd have to go through me before he could get to her. Seemed like a fair arrangement to me. I reached out with my right arm where Whitney should have been and felt the coolness of her side of the bed. My isolated moments were adding up. The flight with the empty seat and now a bed without her. The next day, I'd continue to add to the list. The bourbon distillery tour, then lunch at a great barbecue joint in downtown Louisville. Each activity compounded the fact that my life partner was missing. We capped off the day with the rehearsal dinner, during which my nephew's future ninety-four-year-old grandmother-in-law toasted the soon-to-be-wedded couple and expressed how thankful she was to God for allowing her to live to see this day. At this point, I, and just about everyone else in the room, lost it. Tears streamed down my face as I thought of the simplicity of grandma's gratitude. She had prayed for this day, and God answered her prayers. It reminded me that with prayers, sometimes God says yes, and sometimes God says no.

That Time I Nearly Killed Her

Whitney didn't nag. It was one of many things I loved about her. She knew I was responsible enough to get chores done around the house without having to press. Maybe she needed to do this with her other husbands, but it was completely unnecessary with me, even when it was. Case in point: February of 2010. We had been going out for three years, living together for two. She had been married three times, I once. I wouldn't say that I had become disillusioned with the institution of marriage, but I didn't feel the pressure of having to tie the knot. And that was okay with me until she started dropping hints that it wasn't okay. We had purchased a house in Plymouth with four bedrooms—one for each child and us. It had two fireplaces, an attached two-and-a-half-car garage and an en suite bathroom, which this Iowa boy considered quite luxurious. Her subtle hints eventually became not so subtle. I think she finally said something along the lines of, "Don't you think it would be better for the kids to live in a household where the adults are married?" I got the message—she wanted a proposal, and given the fact that my father had passed away in November 2009, it became clear to me that I shouldn't put important occasions off for too long. So I went online and found a romantic getaway on the North Shore, Cove Point Lodge in Beaver Bay, Minnesota, and booked a room for Valentine's Day weekend. We loaded the car down with treats, booze, lots of warm clothes and my cross-country skis. Although we planned to spend most of the time in our room or around the lodge, I figured we'd make the most of the winter weather and explore one of the state parks during the weekend. I checked several websites and determined that the 9,346 acres of Tettegouche State Park was a good destination, and it wasn't too far north of where we were staying. It's a popular North Shore destination for hikers, climbers, bird watchers, snowmobilers and cross-country skiers. The photos on the website looked intoxicating, and the trails were rated "medium." Perfect.

We reached Cove Point Lodge late in the afternoon on Friday, having delayed our arrival by an hour or so because of the required stop at Betty's Pies in Two Harbors. The shop, which first opened in 1957, is a Minnesota institution situated across Highway 61 from Lake Superior and about 30 miles south of our destination. We walked into the pie shop filled with giddy anticipation and a hunger for something sweet. Half the fun of visiting Betty's is determining exactly which type of pie to get. It reminded me of visiting Baskin-Robbins as a kid—so many choices. Strawberry rhubarb, old-fashioned apple, bumbleberry, blueberry... As we contemplated the two dozen or so choices of pie, inevitably, our conversation would devolve into our usual dessert-defining debate.

"It has to have chocolate in it or it's not dessert," Whitney said, trying to decide between five-layer chocolate cream pie and Butterfinger cream pie. "Fruit is too healthy to be considered a dessert."

"Oh brother, here we go again," I laughed. "Some of the best desserts have fruit in them. Apple crisp. Banana splits. Chocolate cherry cake. And, of course, pie! You are wasting a good pie crust if you don't fill it with fruit."

"Fruit? Where's the decadence? Dessert is about decadence!'

"Fruit can be decadent."

"Hardly. And what about pumpkins or pecans? They're not fruit. You eat them all the time."

"Okay, I grant an exception for pumpkins or sweet potatoes. They're honorary fruits."

"You're crazy."

"No, you're crazy."

By the time the pie showed up at the table, we'd agreed to disagree and focused on the sweet treat before us. A half-hour later, when we arrived at the lodge, we weren't exactly hungry, having filled ourselves at Betty's, but we forced ourselves to eat dinner at the lodge restaurant. Afterward, we relaxed on the leather couches in front of a roaring blaze in the large stone fireplace, enjoying the kind of North Shore winter atmosphere we had hoped for.

The next morning we slept in, got a quick breakfast and then headed south on Highway 61 to take in the frozen glory of Gooseberry Falls State Park. We hiked through the snowy landscape and took photos of ice formations, coniferous trees and each other with our phones. As the winter chill took hold, we decided to change locations, so we returned to our car and headed back up north, stopping at a roadside vendor to rent skis. The operator asked us where we were headed, and when I told him, Tettegouche, he gave me a quizzical look. Even the slightest critical comment could have saved us a lot of grief, but being a descendent of reserved Norwegians, he kept his opinions to himself. We loaded Whitney's rental skis into the car and drove the twenty miles along the picturesque north shore to Tettegouche. At the time, I didn't sense any reluctance from Whitney.

At the trailhead, we put on our skis and began the journey up the trail under cloudy skies and temperatures in the low twenties. If we kept moving, we wouldn't have to worry about the cold at all. We began with a gradual ascent that became a pesky ascent that became an arduous ascent that became a more-challenging-than-we-wanted ascent that became an I-need-a-fucking-sherpa ascent. Stopping several times to catch our breath, wipe our brows and check one of the park's posted trail maps, we agreed that we'd be much happier if the trail started heading downhill as soon as possible. In the not-too-far distance, we heard snowmobilers revving their engines, having a good old time climbing any hills in their path with great ease. Despite being out of her element, Whitney did not whine or nag. She gritted her teeth and endured, possibly thinking that at least this wasn't as painful as childbirth.

After thirty minutes of climbing and several rest breaks, we finally reached the summit. Thank God. It's about time, we agreed. Our aching muscles and creaking bones could finally take a break while gravity did its job and guided us down the hill. The trail was groomed perfectly. All we had to do was place our skis in the tracks and head downhill, which we did for about twelve yards. It was about this time we realized the steepness of the decline. We picked up too much speed, and before we knew it, we were descending at a scary pace. Pines, ash and birch trees rushed by in our periphery vision. If we wanted to avoid concussions—or simply death—we had to stay on the trail, which might have been possible if it was straight rather than zigzagging through the forest.

Before long, we were both leaning back on our skis and crouching down so that if we fell, we wouldn't fall far. As deftly as we possibly could, we leaned over to our left or right and met the ground with as little impact as we could muster. When we had slid to a snowy halt, we would stand up, brush ourselves off and start down the hill again, resorting to this speed escape method time and time again. After five or six bailouts, we'd had enough. "This is ridiculous," Whitney said, exasperated—at the predicament I hoped and not at me. "We're going to break a leg or get killed." I didn't argue. My body felt like I had just gone three rounds with Mike Tyson. I stepped off the trail and jabbed my left binding with the end of my ski pole, then repeated it on my right. Whitney, probably relieved that I agreed that this Nordic adventure was fucked, did the same. We picked up our skis and began walking down the trail, satisfied that this method would allow us to stay upright and, more importantly, not run smack-dab into the middle of a tree. I didn't even worry about encountering other skiers and enduring the recriminating looks that they would inevitably give us. I didn't care. I wanted to live.

Twenty minutes later, we reached the car, packed up the skis and headed back to the ski rental vendor. We didn't exchange a word the entire way. When we got to the rental shop, I went inside by myself. I'm not sure whether Whitney stayed in the car because she was so beat up after our skiing adventure or because she thought I was a complete ass for suggesting that we attempt such a crazy feat in the name of "fun." The vendor recognized me as I placed the skis on the counter. "How'd it go?" he asked mirthfully. Given my aching muscles, bruised pride and angry girlfriend in the SUV, I answered him in true Minnesota fashion, "It was interesting."

Later, at Cove Point Lodge, as the bartender regaled us with her knowledge of tequila and its restorative powers for old people suffering tremendous aches and pains from cross-country skiing, I held Whitney's hand. "I really thought it was an easier trail. I wouldn't have gone on it if I knew it would be that bad."

She smiled genuinely and said, "I know you were not trying to kill me, Dan, but consider this a warning. You get one free pass, and this was it. Don't ever pull something like that on me again." We laughed—me nervously, she maniacally. The tequila worked, as did the dinner and the hot tub afterward. By the time we fell asleep watching Saturday Night Live in the candlelight, our fingers intertwined, I convinced myself that I could indeed go forward with my original plan. She may have wanted to kill me on the trail, but inside the lodge, life had returned to normal.

The next morning after a continental breakfast, which may have included pickled herring because, after all, we were on the North Shore, I suggested that we go for a walk. Whitney scanned the whitecaps on the lake outside the lodge window. The landscape resembled a snow globe that had just been vigorously shaken by a toddler. She gave me a look that said, "Remember, you used up your one free pass yesterday, bud."

"Just a short walk," I promised. "I want to take a picture of the lodge from out on the point, in the snow. It will be cool." She sighed and started to layer up. Although she had been born in Duluth and grew up in the Twin Cities, Whitney never really learned to enjoy winter. It was more a matter of surviving the months between November and March, which made the fact that she had agreed to cross-country ski the day before even more spectacular. After seven layers, she was ready to go.

The snow wasn't too deep, so our Sorels did the trick. We clomped past the fish house, now closed for winter, and headed onto the narrow strip of land that jutted out about a couple hundred yards into the turbulent Lake Superior. There was no clear path, so some of our trek included crawling over large gray boulders. The snow blew sideways off the lake into our reddening faces. I was beginning to rethink my plan. Was I stupid? Didn't she make it very clear that of the four seasons, she rated winter fifth? Maybe she suspected what I was up to, or maybe she felt like she had no other choice but to do exactly what the crazy Iowan suggested. We were about halfway out onto the point when our progress was blocked by large conifers, even larger boulders and no clear path. Thinking this was as good a place as any other, I turned and bent down to one knee. It was here, in the sideways snow, with a rosy face, numb lips and frozen fingers, I professed my love for her and asked if she would do me the honor of becoming my wife. She gasped a little (apparently, it was somewhat of a surprise), wiped the snot from her nose with the back of her mitten and smiled, "Of course."

I had tried to kill her the day before. I forced her to take a frozen walk on a frozen Valentine's Day morning. I had no ring. And she still said yes. Either my magnetism was overwhelming, or she had no willpower. My plan, though seemingly disastrous, worked like a charm.

Routine from Hell

After I returned from Louisville, we settled into a routine. Normally, I love routines. I thrive off them. They get me through the day. They create order in an otherwise frenzied life. Unfortunately, this chemo/battling cancer routine was not a good kind of routine. It seemed more like paddling a canoe upstream at the edge of a giant waterfall. It didn't matter that your arms were getting tired, you had to keep paddling or else you'd go right over the falls, and then you'd be fucked.

Every other Tuesday morning, I'd drive Whitney to Minnesota Oncology for chemotherapy. Whitney listened to her podcast while the poison coursed through her veins, searching for cancerous cells to kill. I tried my best to block out the surroundings by listening to classical music and answering work emails. I had to do something to block out the madness that surrounded us. Whenever I'd take out my air buds, I'd hear Mr. Packer going on and on about Aaron Rodgers' latest amazing feat or the incessant chatter of talking heads on Fox News paying homage to their exalted leader.

Visits to the infusion center were to be endured as if marching off to war. During her second round of chemo on

September 11—a day that depressed everyone—Whit had a reaction to her pharmaceutical cocktail. A few minutes after getting hooked up to her IV, Whitney said she felt overheated, which I relayed to the care team, and within seconds the nurse swooped in and remedied the situation by adding Benadryl to her medication. Whitney said it made her feel "floaty and nice." Floaty and nice enough to continue the treatment without further incident. In the past, something like this would have freaked me out to the point where I would have to get up and walk around to work out the bad thoughts racing through my head. Oh my God, she's going to die. The meds are killing her. What the hell… But abnormality had become normal. People jabbing things into her, ports, IVs, hypodermic needles, grafts, etc., were just part of the cancer world to which I had become numb. I simply put my air buds back into my ears and cranked the Brahms.

The next day, before the aftershocks of the latest chemo treatment kicked in and while she still had the slightest hint of energy, Whitney decided to take the offensive with her hair. She knew it was just a matter of time before she would have to part ways with her beautiful mane. While I had seen photos of a younger Whitney with shorter hair, I had only known her when it was long. I loved how it framed her smile and tickled my face whenever she leaned over me for a kiss. Every time she had an inch taken off to make it more manageable, I silently winced and lied that "I like it like that." As I headed off to work, she warned me that she'd look different when I returned. I manufactured a smile and said, "You'll look beautiful no matter what." A few hours later, she went to her stylist and had it buzzed close to her skull, then dyed what was left of it purple once she got home.

"It's going to be so much easier to maintain," she told me when I got home later that day. "But you already know that, right?"

"Haha, yes," I said, running my palm across my bald pate.

Although she made jokes, it was no laughing matter. She knew that she could no longer hide the fact that she was battling cancer when she ventured out into public. She could have purchased a wig and hid it from those with less discerning eyes, but she never considered that an option. She took one look at the wig catalog they had given her at the Piper Center and quickly decided that she'd either go with the buzz cut or a headscarf. If anybody didn't like it, they could go to hell.

* * *

Along with lethargy, nausea and hair loss, chemotherapy does a number on white blood cells. As a result, patients need to get an injection of Neulasta, which helps stimulate the growth of new cells. After her first chemo session, Whitney went back to the clinic the next day to receive the shot. After the second session, we decided it would be a lot easier if we administered the shot at home and cut out the middleman. Because of a work conflict, I was not available to give her the shot at the prescribed time (twenty-five hours after chemo), so her mother drove up from Rosemount to jab her eldest daughter with a needle. A few days later, on September 17, Whitney added the following to her CaringBridge site, providing a sense of her thoughts on chemo:

> Whew—so things get real quiet around
> here during chemo week. Mostly, Daisy

and I snooze all the live long day, and toss and turn a good chunk of the night. It's frustrating to be so walloped that I literally wouldn't be able to walk around the block (though let's be honest, I haven't set out on any treks recently!) Not to be overly cheerleader-y but I'm convinced this chemo is super powerful, and that's why it really packs a punch.

But it's now NOT chemo week! And I'm super excited that I met with our neighborhood herbalist today. She's set me up with all kinds of boosters, specifically to address the nausea, lack of energy, and supporting my immune system into healing my bod. There's mushrooms x3, magnesium, vitamin B complex, vitamin D, and the most serious medicine in the form of Fu Zheng, a customized blend of herbs and stuff. It's simmering on the stove right now...I'm not going to lie, it smells more like medicine than a comforting tea. But I'll be happy to gulp down a cup every day! I'm hoping it'll help me rebound from the chemo treatments faster, and also support my body healing itself. Grateful for Jessie's expertise, and my oncologist being open to this additional protocol.

That fall, Whitney made several trips to see Jessie, the herbalist, whose store was just a five-minute walk away from our house. Whitney was game to try just about anything to settle her stomach, ease the pain or kick the tumors' asses. She ended up stockpiling quite a bit of these non-medicinal concoctions, and soon our kitchen resembled a smaller version of the herbalist store. If it helped her cope, I was all in. Several people came forward with offers to provide her with cannabis, be it procured illegally in Minnesota or legally in Colorado and then illegally transported here. Her oncologist suggested medical cannabis and cleared the way for her to participate in Minnesota's state-run program. When the law passed in 2014, the medical association for which I work lobbied hard to keep physicians away from the troublesome parts of the law—namely, to avoid having them "prescribe" the federally forbidden substance. As passed, the Minnesota law calls for a physician to acknowledge that their patient has one of the qualifying conditions (cancer is at the top of the list). Then it's up to the patient to fill out the paperwork and register with the state. The patient needs to procure the medication at one of only a handful of distribution centers across Minnesota. Fortunately, we were only a short drive from one in St. Paul. The restrictive nature of Minnesota's program at the time prohibited the use of the raw plant form, so you couldn't just buy a joint and smoke that. Instead, you had to either vape it, ingest it as a liquid, spray it under your tongue or apply it as a topical. Because I was Whitney's caretaker, I had to fill out the paperwork as well and prove to the state that I was not some kind of Walter White planning to build a drug empire with the medical cannabis meant for my wife.

    Although Whitney and I had smoked our share of weed during our lives, we never consumed it together. By the time we met, that ship had sailed. We knew what to expect of marijuana when we were young, but the drug had become more potent over the years, so we decided to stick to what we knew, and that was the buzz of alcohol. Nonetheless, it seemed weird to be driving over to St. Paul to legally buy pot. They call it medicinal, and everything is on the up and up, but when we entered the clinic, it felt to me, at least, anything but. Maybe it's just my imagination, but most of the patients seemed paranoid, acting like they were doing something against the law. Eyes darted back and forth or focused on the floor, anywhere but on the other patients. The woman at the front desk reminded me of the sullen goth girls back in college who I learned to avoid. She asked Whitney to fill out additional paperwork and told us that we would be summoned when it was time to meet with a consultant.

"Is it just me, or do you feel like DEA agents might bust through the front door at any moment?" I joked as Whit filled out the required forms.

"It's just you. Paranoid much?"

I sat there silently and thought about my history of cannabis use, thinking that if you asked the seventeen-year-old version of me if he thought that one day the drug would be legal, he would have put down his bag of Doritos and flicked you in the forehead with an orange finger. I thought about the first time I got high, in the park across from my friend Coop's house. I had expected that the effect would be instant after I inhaled my first puff and then complained that I didn't feel anything right before it hit me. We seemed to float across the street as we headed back into Coop's house to get something to eat and drink. Then I thought about the first time we smoked hashish, and Coop described how it expands in your lungs. I didn't know whether that was true, but it just about blew my mind when I imagined it happening. Then I thought about one fateful night in the autumn of 1981 when I learned that the Man didn't want you to enjoy any Mary Jane.

Like many Friday nights during high school, my friends and I focused on partying. Coop, Craig, Tommy, Chewy, Barry and I stood in the parking lot of the Annie Wittenmyer Home smoking dope out of a cherry-red three-foot bong and drinking Miller Lite that Coop's older sister had bought for us. Annie Wittenmyer had been a champion of the downtrodden who opened a free school for underprivileged kids in Keokuk, Iowa, advocated for Civil War orphans and helped create new orphanages, including the Iowa Soldiers' Orphan's Home that would be named for her in 1949.

Joining us dudes were a couple of female classmates who had consumed a few beers too many. Barry gallantly offered to drive them home, perhaps thinking that some serious necking was in his future. Like the girls, Barry wasn't exactly sober, so I figured those of us who stayed behind were dodging a bullet by not getting into a car with those three. As soon as they drove out of the parking lot and turned right, a Davenport Police squad car approached from the left and drove slowly by the entrance to the lot. Tommy, the only other person with a car that night, suggested that we either skedaddle or risk being sitting ducks for the cops if they decided to come back to investigate. The five of us quickly piled into his father's Delta 88 while Tommy dumped the water out of the bong and stowed it under the front seat. He cranked the ignition, put it into drive and drove it across East 29th Street into Garfield Park. He clicked off the lights, and there we sat, some one hundred yards from where we were just seconds ago.

"Hey, Tommy. Don't you think we should get completely out of here?" I asked. "All we did was cross the street."

"Nah. We were in the light over there," he said in his deep baritone, motioning to the streetlights in the Wittenmyer parking lot. "We're in the dark over here."

"We're in the dark. Alone. In a parking lot one hundred yards from where we just were. You don't think they'll see us over here?" I asked incredulously from the back seat. Chewy and Craig, on either side of me, nodded vigorously.

Tommy, being behind the wheel, had a little more power over what we would do next. "The cop already drove by. If they were going to stop, they would have stopped already. He's probably at the end of his shift, and the last thing he wants to do is fill out a bunch of paperwork on a group of punks like us."

Coop, riding shotgun, nodded. "Yeah, maybe what Tommy said."

"Sure," I agreed, "but is it worth the gamble?" No sooner had I uttered the words when we saw a cop, perhaps the same one, probably the same one, driving south on Eastern Avenue, looking as if he would turn onto 29th Street.

Tommy put the car into drive and turned right onto 29th Street, half a block in front of the police car. Hearts hammered inside of young chests. *This is not good*, my conscience repeated. Suddenly, the interior of the Delta 88 was awash with red light. *Oh, shit.* Tommy continued to drive under the speed limit for half a block until the cop bleeped the siren. Tommy turned onto the first street off 29th and pulled over to the curb. We all had at least a beer or two in us as well as copious amounts of THC, but with that red light filling the interior of the car and a real live, breathing police officer behind us, we sobered up rather quickly. Well, most of us. "We was sittin' ducks for the policeman," Coop sang quietly, recalling the lyrics from one of our favorite bands at the time—Van Halen. A few of us laughed.

"Quiet, guys," Tommy snapped. "Everybody just be cool, you hear?" After several long, agonizing minutes, the cop approached the car.

"Okay, boys, I need to see some IDs first off," said the officer, who, much to our surprise—being a bunch of sexist seventeen-year-olds—turned out to be a woman. She stood just outside Tommy's window, waiting patiently for us to get our shit together. We fumbled through our pockets and produced our Iowa driver's licenses, which we eagerly handed to Tommy, who in turn placed them into the police officer's waiting palm.

Tommy, whose deep voice now resembled honey straight from the hive, asked, "May I ask, Officer Hamilton," he said, reading her nametag, "why you are pulling us over?"

She, I'm sure, bit her tongue. Wasn't it obvious to the entire world why she pulled us over? Guilt was written in 36-point font all over our faces. "What were you boys doing back there in the park? A little partying?"

"Oh no, ma'am, we weren't partying. We were just listening to some music." Tommy looked at the rest of us, who replied with nodding heads.

"I can smell the pot, uh, Tommy," she said, reading his license. She flipped through the rest of them, taking her time to see what she was up against—a hapless bunch of nerdy, white, privileged seventeen-year-olds who were too stupid to find a more concealed place to drink warm beer and smoke dope. "Okay, I'm going to need you to step out of the vehicle. All of you. If you don't have anything on you, I'll think about letting you go with a warning, so don't try anything stupid, understand?"

I certainly understood. At this point, I would do just about anything—jumping jacks, handstands, somersaults—to avoid going downtown. We all climbed out of the car and stood between it and the sidewalk, each of us glancing around a) to see if anyone was watching us from their homes, witnessing one of the most embarrassing moments of our young lives, or b) scoping out possible escape routes. I know the thought certainly crossed my mind. There were five of us and only one cop. She couldn't chase us all down. The thought didn't linger in my brain for too long, though. I wouldn't be able to return to Central High on Monday if word got out that I ran off and abandoned my friends. News like that would have circulated through the halls before the first bell rang, so we acted like obedient children while the cop quickly and loosely frisked us. None of us had anything on our persons other than wallets and car keys. Officer Hamilton then moved on to Tommy's car and, after a brief search, found the bong under the front seat. "I assume this is what you used to smoke it?" We all nodded. "Okay, here's what we're going to do. We are all going to get into the squad car while I run your licenses to make sure you don't have any priors. If you come up clean, I can probably let you go with a warning. Only if you come up clean, understand?" Five heads nodded in unison.

She obviously knew how freaked out we were and that we did not appear to pose a threat, so she let Tommy sit up front while the rest of us crammed into the back of the squad car. After she received confirmation that we were clean as whistles, she turned to us and said, "Okay, somewhere on you guys, because I didn't find it in the car, is your stash. Hand that over and you'll be free to go."

After some hemming and hawing, Chewy reached down into his waistband and pulled out a plastic sandwich bag filled with a couple of inches of weed—no frisk would ever produce that, which he certainly knew. He handed it up to her and sat back, dejected.

"Okay, good. You guys have been cooperative so far. You have clean sheets. You look like you've learned your lesson." We all nodded vigorously to this. I could taste freedom. Soon, we'd be walking home, and our parents would never be the wiser. Tommy would have to explain to his parents why the car was left behind because we all assumed the cop wouldn't let us drive away, even though we all felt completely sober at this point. "Okay. Since the baggie of pot got by me the first time I frisked you, I need you guys to tell me that you have nothing else on you. Anyone else have some weed hidden in their waistlines? Anything like that?"

Of course not, I thought. Chewy had supplied the weed that night. My heart rate returned to normal and my breathing eased. And then it happened. Coop spoke almost inaudibly, "Well, I have…"

"I'm sorry, speak up," Officer Hamilton said sternly. "What did you say?"

My heart started to sprint again. Coop cleared his throat. "I've got a hit of acid," he said, digging deep into the front right pocket of his jeans. First, he pulled out a piece of lint. Then, after further excavation, he produced a tiny, tiny piece of foil, which contained a microscopic hit of acid. You could practically feel the collective air escaping our lungs.

Officer Hamilton slowly shook her head. "Aww, for the love of Pete. So close, so close," she said to herself and then addressed us. "Okay, I'm going to have to take you in. You guys weren't up front with me."

For a brief second, I thought about begging her to let us go. Or at least just me. I didn't know about the acid.

Coop hadn't mentioned it all. Hell, I never ever tried it or had any intention to, ever. I shouldn't be punished. I was anti-acid. But then I decided the guys would likely call me a pussy later and possibly ostracize me, so I kept my trap shut. Officer Hamilton put the cruiser into gear and drove us downtown to the police station, where we sat in a holding cell until our parents arrived. Because of that humiliating night, I didn't touch pot until well into my junior year of college.

Now, some thirty-five years later, I was in the process of buying cannabis legally. After Whit filled out the paperwork at the dispensary, they buzzed us into the back section of the operation, where several patients waited to either meet with a consultant or pick up their latest supply. We took a seat, and once again, I surveyed the room expecting, quite ignorantly, to see a bunch of ponytailed hippies wearing Phish T-shirts, puka shells, cargo pants and Birkenstocks. While there may have been one or two of those, the rest of the patients represented all walks of life—old, young, poor, well-off, Black, Hmong, white and everyone else you might find in the Twin Cities. Obviously, I needed to take this more seriously. After all, this wasn't some kind of street deal; this was legitimate medicine. The cannabis would help Whitney cope with her pain and increase her appetite, both of which she certainly needed.

After a ten-minute wait, we were summoned to a room off the main waiting area to meet with an administrator who told us about the state's program and the various products the lab had available. We were then joined by a pharmacist who provided more details on what each of the products was designed to do. Armed with plenty of information, we decided that Whit would benefit from a THC-heavy oral suspension that she'd take before bed. This would help with the pain and allow her to sleep longer. We also agreed that she would use a vape pen a few minutes before each meal to help with her appetite. After selecting these two forms of cannabis, we were given a prescription, which the clinic staff filled in a different area off the main waiting room. A wall of thick (and, I'm assuming, bulletproof) glass separated those filling the orders and the patients. It all felt very Fort Knox-ish to me.

We left the lab with Whit's prescription in a paper bag as if we had just visited the store for a loaf of bread and a gallon of milk. The gray skies and a cold wind hurried us along to the car. As I buckled in and started the engine, I let out a sigh. Our lives had changed so much over the past few months that it seemed like we were occupying other people's bodies. Whitney reached over and grabbed my hand. We sat there for a moment.

"Thanks for coming with me," she said.

"Of course, how could I pass up the opportunity to buy pot legally for the first time? At age fifty-five?"

"I know this is all difficult for you."

"You're the one with cancer."

"But still…"

"I love you."

"I love you more."

I smiled. She loved to say that to me. Generally, Whitney was not a competitive person except when it came to two areas—playing racquetball and saying "I love you" the most sincerely. We played racquetball for a few years until our bodies kept reminding us that we were no longer young. At that point, our desire to compete turned to less strenuous measures, like seeing who could tell the other they loved them more. Whitney always won. My strategy was to catch her by surprise. Hers was persistence until she started using the "I love you more" approach. I had never heard it until I met Whitney. I'd sneak in a subtle "I love you" as I walked by her after mowing the lawn, figuring that such an unromantic setting matched by my unromantic perspiration would take her off guard. She'd smile, peck the only part of my cheek not festooned with grass clippings and say, "I love you more." Unfair! How do you respond to that without sounding like a petulant child? "Oh yeah? Well, I love you more than that. To infinity and beyond!"

Not that long ago, I came across a promo for a red T-shirt as I flipped through a pre-Valentine's Day circular in the Sunday paper. Written in white across the front of the shirt were the words "Love you more." It was as if Whitney, knowing how much I ached for her a year after her passing, had conspired with the folks at Target to place that T-shirt there just to let me know that she was still around, watching me.

Now when I tell her I love her, I don't hear a reply. So, I guess, in a way, I eventually won that competition.

Halloween Hospital

Three months into her cancer battle, the healthcare team wanted to see how the first four rounds of chemo had affected Hannibal, Buffalo Bill, Ted Bundy, et al. So, on October 21, 2019, Whitney went in for another PET scan in which they injected her with "radioactive sugar to 'light up' the active cells," as she described it in her un-doctorly manner on CaringBridge. The results, Dr. T explained, were mixed. The good news was that the tumor in her spine (Bundy) had been eradicated, as were some of the small lesions on her left lung. However, Hannibal—the original asshole, the fuck-nuts who started this whole sad chapter, had not been affected at all, and the lymph node in her left breast had also grown.

The day after this disappointing news, we headed back to the chemo lab for Whitney's fifth round and a new concoction of chemicals, which her oncologist said would be less invasive. Whitney's first round of chemo had included sessions every other Tuesday for eight weeks; this new regimen called for chemo every week for three months. Whit was optimistic that this chemo would result in less nausea and more energy. Three days after the fifth round, though, she felt feverish. Given her compromised immune system, we knew we had to be on the lookout for infection, so we headed into Abbott. This turned into a six-day stay so the care team could treat the strep infection in her left breast.

Abbott, which began in a small house in 1882, sits smack-dab in the middle of Minneapolis, making it equally accessible to all parts of the city. It began as Northwestern Hospital, created to care for the women and children of the milling city. One of the hospital's early employees, Dr. Amos Abbott, left after twenty years and started another hospital for women just blocks away. Abbott and Northwestern hospitals merged in 1970, consolidating into a single location at Chicago and Twenty-seventh Avenues in 1980. Today the facility is the largest not-for-profit hospital in the Twin Cities. *U.S. News and World Report* regularly ranks it among "America's Best Hospitals" in the country. We were lucky to have such a top-notch facility only fifteen minutes away from our home, but we didn't feel so lucky when her stay lasted nearly a week. We were reminded that cancer doesn't give a shit about your plans. It's like that old Yiddish adage, "Man plans, God laughs," but instead, it's "Man plans, cancer says 'fuck you, I'll ruin all of your plans, you schlub, because I can.'"

It wasn't Whitney's first trip to Abbott, and it certainly wouldn't be her last.

She pointed out on her CaringBridge site that the last time she had spent an overnight at the hospital, she was giving birth to her only child, Sam. "I'm real glad I'm not having a baby this time," she wrote. Frankly, I wish she was.

For the week leading up to Halloween, I visited Whitney in the morning before work. Shirley would come in to spend the day, and I'd return after work. Whit had a single room but never felt alone because either her mother or I was there. And there was the constant stream of the healthcare team—nurses, hospitalists, infectious disease physicians, palliative care docs, sanitation crew, cafeteria workers… How anyone can get anything more than a nap in with all the interruptions is beyond me. As a result, cracks began to appear in Whitney's optimistic facade, and after six days in a strange place getting poked and prodded with very little sleep, she could no longer hide her frazzled state.

"I don't know how I'm going to keep this up," she told me upon her release from the hospital on Halloween afternoon.

"We'll get through it. Together," I said, squeezing her hand.

"Speaking of getting through stuff," she said, squeezing my hand back, "I don't know if I have the energy to have a bunch of kids stopping by tonight. Can we just sit this one out this year?"

Shit. I had done nothing to prepare for the evening's parade of ghosts, goblins, witches and Power Rangers. "There's no candy at home," I said at a stoplight. "No candy bars or anything. I think you're right. We'd be better off just turning off the porch light and skipping Halloween this year." Honestly, I just wanted to retreat to the bedroom and watch crappy Halloween movies. It wasn't much of a holiday, but at least Whit was back home and by my side.

Before turning off the bedroom light for the night, I prepared to give her a shot of her latest medicine. Her bedside table looked like a cluttered pharmacy, with a variety of orange prescription bottles, most of which were filled with painkillers. Over the course of her battle, she got to know (and often hate) Dilaudid, morphine, methadone, letrozole, Zofran and various steroids. Following her six-day stay at the hospital, we added Lovenox, an anticoagulant to prevent blood clots, to the mix. Twice a day, we needed to inject her abdomen with the med. The nurses had demonstrated to us how to administer it before we left the hospital with the idea that either one of us could do it.

"Okay," I said, rubbing alcohol on her belly. "I won't always be around to give you a shot, so you're going to have to do it yourself sometimes."

"I don't know if I can," she said, looking away as I unwrapped the individually packaged hypodermic needle pre-filled with the blood thinner.

"Sure you can," I said, pinching an inch of her belly fat.

"I couldn't do it with the bone marrow stimulator," she said, referring to the shot her aunt and mother had administered after her early chemo sessions.

"Yeah, but that was just a couple of times," I said. "You need to take this med twice a day for who knows how long." I jabbed her belly at an angle and pushed the plunger down until all the medicine had been dispensed, then pulled the hypodermic out and pushed the plunger down again, which released a safety guard around the needle. We finished the ritual off with a kiss. "Thank you," she said, knowing that sticking a needle into her belly twice a day was low on my list of things I liked to do for my spouse.

She knew I was no fan of needles. As a kid, I turned away every time a nurse administered a shot on some TV medical drama or some drug addict shot up in a movie. I knew it was fake, but just the thought of it was enough to make me woozy. Even today, nearing sixty, I ask the nurse if it's okay to lie down whenever I have blood drawn at my annual check-up. It's been years since I felt lightheaded getting blood drawn, but I figure it's better safe than sorry, and I know that the last thing nurses want to deal with is some grown man keeling over while they're trying to take a few ccs of blood. So, I didn't relish the idea of having to jab my wife, but you can overcome quite a bit for love. The first few times, my heart pounded, and my hand shook, but we got through it. That's easy for me to say, though, as I wasn't the one getting punctured. After a few weeks of this routine, I gave up on trying to convince Whitney to self-administer. She argued that if the roles were reversed, I would not be able to give myself a shot, and I couldn't argue. So every morning before I left for work and every evening before bedtime, I injected her with the blood thinner. I didn't like it, but I loved Whitney, and I would overcome it for her.

    I can certainly see how the caretaker role wears people down. It certainly frayed my nerves, but I didn't have a choice, nor would I have it any other way. In a way, Whitney was lucky. Not that she got fast-moving cancer, obviously, but that she had someone to be there to help her on her journey. And frankly, that's what scares the hell out of me. Whitney and I thought we'd be together until well into our eighties, and although it was never stated, we both figured it would be me who would die first. After all, both of her parents were still alive. Cancer had not been an issue in her family. My father had diabetes, high blood pressure, high cholesterol and Parkinson's. My mom died of a heart attack. My grandparents had battled cancer and heart attacks. Surely more than high cholesterol waits for me.

    And yet, I'm the survivor.

    The situation reminds me of a song by a favorite band of mine, Death Cab for Cutie. In "What Sarah Said," the first part of the narrative is that of a young man watching his lover die in a hospital. The last lines of the sobering song keep repeating, "So who's going to watch you die?" This is from the point of view of the dying lover, who is urging the one she's leaving behind to find love again and not to spend the rest of his time mourning her loss. "Fall in love again, so that you will have someone to watch you die," she is essentially saying. It's difficult to listen to the song anymore because I can't help but think, who's going to watch me die?

When it Rains, it Floods

Given that we had both been married before, the deliberations over our wedding were relatively painless. Some couples really test the strengths of their relationship when it comes to these types of decisions (style of invitation, reception location, DJ vs. live band, flavor of cake, etc.) Not us. Whitney and I had both walked away from the Catholic church, so having it in some ostentatious cathedral was out of the question. We didn't think it would feel right to tie the knot in a church, although I doubt God cared that we were only occasional churchgoers. Instead, we turned our focus to an outdoor venue. As members of the 1,200-acre University of Minnesota Landscape Arboretum in beautiful Carver County, we had ready access to the perfect locale. We decided that the ideal time to get married would be on the third anniversary of our first date—June 25—when we enjoyed lunch on the deck at Lord Fletcher's, and I discovered her tattoo. It also happened to be a Friday, so we set the time for six and began filling in the details.

We met with representatives from the Arboretum, toured the grounds for potential ceremony spots and eventually decided on the rose garden because of its tall white fencing that would afford the wedding party a little privacy in an otherwise busy park filled with stressed-out parents desperate for someplace to take their kids for an hour or two. The surrounding flowers were beautiful, of course, and there was a nice fountain. It would be a small, brief affair, so we didn't need a lot of room. I asked my friend, Eddie, to perform the ceremony. (Recovering Catholics are as leery of clergy as they are of churches and nuns.) Eddie assured me that he was an official pastor, even whipping out the divinity card he received from some church online. He had the power to wed and had done it before. He bragged that the one couple he had married was still together, so he was one-for-one. An enviable batting average.

We wrote our vows, worked with another friend to design invitations and asked Whitney's sister, a passionate shutterbug, to take photos. Most of our time and attention went toward the reception, which we would host at our Plymouth home. The plan called for having the immediate family over after the wedding and then hold the big reception/party the following night. With an expected crowd of one hundred people, we felt the pressure of making sure everyone had a good time or at least were provided with the ingredients to have a good time if they chose. We painted, we cleaned, we trimmed bushes, we bought plenty of booze and paid a couple of friends to cater it. We even washed the dog. We wanted it to be a reception that people remembered for years to come.

As the big day approached, all the pieces fell into place except for the one thing we could not control—the weather. Being late June in Minnesota, we could have faced a variety of climate curveballs, from snow to blazing heat to tornadoes. As it turns out, in 2010, Mother Nature gave us the climate of central Florida—the kind that produces swamp ass. On the bright side, we didn't have to wear the wedding parkas we had picked out.

On the day of the wedding, we arrived at the Arboretum an hour before the ceremony was to take place. The heat and humidity combo made us feel like we were strolling through a sauna. The dark sky to the west mocked us as we inspected the Rose Garden site. "Do you think this is going to work?" I asked my wife-to-be, who walked in the high heels of an optimist. "I think so. Let's go find our contact at the Arboretum office. He said we should check in when we got here." I looked to the west again. I didn't hear any rumbles coming out of the skies, but I didn't hear any robins singing either. We walked over to the main building, where we were greeted by a wall of perfectly chilled, humidity-free air as we walked through the double doors. The look on Whitney's face mirrored what I was thinking, "Oh my God, it is so much more comfortable in here."

Brian, with the Arboretum staff, greeted us with a smile marred by a look of concern. "Nice to see you," he said as he ushered us into a backroom where two computer monitors displayed the local radar. Any meteorologist would have felt at home.

"How's it looking? Can we get the ceremony in?" I asked Brian, full of hope. "It's going to be short." Brevity was something Whitney and I had agreed upon. Yes, we loved each other. Yes, we wanted this to be a day everyone would remember. Yes, some of our family members traveled hundreds of miles, and many of them were diehard romantics, but a fifteen-minute wedding would do the trick in our eyes, the state of Minnesota and, we hoped, our more traditional family members.

With one hand, Brian scratched his chin. With the other, he pointed to a green blob on the computer screen.

"This cell looks quite active and appears to be heading right for us. It may not strike until after six but is it worth taking the chance?"

"Well, it's only rain," I offered, trying to play the optimist but not even convincing myself.

"I don't know," Brian said, rubbing his hands together in a very Lady Macbeth-like fashion. "This looks like more than just rain. Could produce hail or even worse—tornadic activity." Okay, who was this guy, Minnesota's answer to Al Roker? "It looks like it could get pretty nasty out there."

Whitney and I excused ourselves and went into the main area of the building, an expansive hall filled with educational displays of flora and fauna. Large windows allowed plenty of natural light to fill the space. It wasn't the same as being outside but closer than most buildings. Could we hold the ceremony here? By six, the Arboretum would be closed to the general public, so we didn't have to worry about the Olson family from Albert Lea wandering through while we got hitched. Through the large windows, we could see the wind picking up. The dark sky threatened to open at any minute and unleash a torrent of Biblical proportion. But, then again, anyone living in the Midwest long enough knows that it could be dark and ominous one moment and sunny and beautiful the next. "What do you want to do, Whit? I get the sense that Brian wants us to move it inside. But it's our wedding. We get to decide."

Whitney couldn't hide her disappointment. The Rose Garden would have been such a picturesque backdrop for our nuptials and photos, but we also didn't want to melt in the humidity, get pelted with toaster-sized hail or get sucked up into a twister like Dorothy Gale. "I guess we should probably move it inside," she said finally. "Stupid weather. I really wanted to get married in the garden."

"I know, babe. Weather is stupid."

As our family members arrived, several of them were openly relieved that we weren't going to make them stand out in the humidity. As Online Pastor Eddie began the ceremony, I looked past him at the sky, which had turned black. In the distance, to the north, it appeared that the world was coming to an end. Meanwhile, the pavement remained dry at the Arboretum. Fifteen minutes later, we were wed, papers had been signed and we were ready to head home for dinner and drinks. Stepping outside, I couldn't help but feel a bit disappointed. Yes, it was windier than the opening scenes of *The Wizard of Oz*, and the heat and humidity felt like the top of a boiling pot of pasta, but the rain had held off. We could have gotten married in the Rose Garden after all. We'd be swimming in our own perspiration, but we could have done it. Damn it.

As Whitney and I headed into the parking lot, Lily offered to drive us home. We weren't drinking yet, but she figured it was our wedding day, so why not play the role of chauffeur. Everyone climbed into their respective vehicles, and we started the wagon train back to Plymouth. Above us, the dark clouds continued to swirl, and we wondered at what point the rain would begin. By the time Lily piloted our Durango onto northbound Interstate 494, the skies opened, and it was as if God, or those who work for him, had opened a million fire hydrants. Cautious drivers pulled over to the side of the road while Lily pressed on, slowing down enough so she could see where we were going. Eventually, we got to our turnoff and made our way to Sunset Trail, which led home. We had slowed down considerably, but the rain kept intensifying finally to the point when we were less than a quarter mile from our house. Lily had to pull over. We couldn't see the front of the car.

I gripped Whitney's hand. "Isn't there an old wives' tale about when it rains on your wedding day, you'll have a stormy marriage?" I asked, joking, while we waited for the rain to let up.

"You're thinking of that Alanis Morrisette song," she said, pulling her phone out of her purse.

"Actually, I wasn't," I said. "That may be the stupidest song I've ever heard. I don't ever want to think of that song. In fact, the ironic thing about that song is she doesn't have a fucking clue of what irony is." I started to mock-sing, "It's like rain on your wedding day. It's a free ride when you've already paid…"

Whitney, reading her phone, interrupted me, for the sake of her and Lily's sanity. "According to this, rain is actually good luck on your wedding day."

"Unless you're driving in it," Lily chimed in.

"It means your marriage is going to last."

After a couple minutes, the rain lightened up enough for us to see again, and Lily drove the rest of the way home. When everyone else had gathered at the house, and we sat down for dinner, the other drivers shared their harrowing tales of driving through the Great Downpour of 2010. Over the course of the weekend, we received more than three inches of rain. The white tents we had erected in the front yard to protect our reception guests from the sun went unused because the rain dropped so hard, and the wind blew so blustery that if you stood in the middle of the tent, you'd still get wet. In the crawl space underneath our living room, where our guests were jammed in elbow to elbow, our two sump pumps ran nearly non-stop, keeping the water out of the basement. Years afterward, whenever the topic of our wedding came up, the conversation would quickly turn to the weather. It made us smile to think that our nuptials were now legendary for our family and friends. Never mind the fact that the reason they remembered it so clearly is that they feared they would drown driving to our home.

Okay, So the Chemo Didn't Work

In early November 2019, the days got both literally and figuratively darker. After consulting with Dr. J, the surgeon, Dr. T decided to change course. The chemo treatment, they determined, had failed. Hannibal, the original tumor in her breast, and Dahmer, her burgeoning lymph node, appeared to be unfazed by the magic chemicals they had pumped into her body over the past three and a half months.

"Motherfucker," I said quietly upon getting the news from Whitney. We sat on our turquoise, mid-century modern couch in our living room. Around us, the dog and cat paced, wondering why dinner was late.

"We still have radiation," she offered. "They'll just zap Hannibal and his crew."

"I know," I said, hugging her carefully, not to add to her pain. "But when you are battling cancer, you want as many tools at your disposal as possible, and now we're down one."

"I know," she said into my chest.

Losing chemo, the treatment that has proven to be the most successful with so many other cancer patients took our breath and words away. We held each other silently, lost in our own dark places.

In the next day or two, Dr. T pulled some strings, and, in short order, the healthcare team had Whitney set up to start radiation. On November 13, she began daily radiation treatments, with the plan calling for four to six weeks of treatments. We didn't think much about it at the time (we were grateful for the speed at which the wheels were spinning in the sometimes-lethargic world of healthcare), but looking back now, we should have realized that the speed was based on need. Desperate need. The healthcare team needed to make progress on Hannibal and Dahmer before it was too late. Maybe Whitney knew and just didn't share it with me, but I, at that time, still had faith in the system and that my God would not take away the love of my life.

Abbott Northwestern's Radiation Oncology Department is tucked away down an alley across the street from the Minnesota Oncology chemo lab we grew to know so well. It's almost like it's being hidden away from the world as if they're worried that passers-by might decide to break in late at night to get a shot of radiation. For the chemo appointments, we parked our car in a large parking ramp and had a short hike to get into the clinic. For radiation, we parked fifteen to twenty feet from the entrance. Treatments were short, so patients moved in and out at a rapid pace. Treatments except for the first one, that is. Our initial visit to radiation was anything but quick. The healthcare team had to make marks on her so that the daily treatments could be done efficiently. Since they are blasting you with a laser, they need to be as accurate as possible; it's all about precision. When you enter the radiation department, you are greeted by two admins who check you in and give you a UPC code which they can use to track you. Across from the front desk hangs a large bell that patients clang when they have finished their therapy regimen. It's a "good riddance" bell. If all went well, in four to six weeks, Whitney would whack that son of a bitch.

After checking in, I'd sit in one of the twenty-four or so chairs in the waiting room, and Whitney would head off to the locker room to put on her gown and bathrobe. She'd return and join me, where we would normally sit quietly and wait for a tech to come out and get her for treatment. The waiting room was never empty, but it certainly had fewer patients than the chemo lab. Unlike the chemo lab, radiation had no food. Get in and get out seemed to be their motto.

Like Minnesota Oncology, we became familiar with the various clientele at the radiation lab but never really talked to them. Perhaps, it was because of the transitory nature of the treatment or, more likely, radiation patients are more burdened with reality to take the time to interact with their fellow patients. Chemo comes first, and when that doesn't work, they ship you over to radiation, so it's obvious that things aren't going so well. Not that you are ever optimistic when you are told you have cancer, but you certainly must be a little more positive when you haven't already tried something and had it fail. I didn't blame anyone in that waiting room for keeping to themselves. They deserved their privacy. However, Whitney and I both wistfully noticed one family in particular. Mom, dad, healthy son, cancer-stricken son. Both boys were under five. Can you imagine having to comfort the sick boy and counsel the healthy one? The anguish. The tempered optimism. It broke our hearts every time we saw that little boy come in with his family. What a way to start off a life.

Whitney quickly settled into the new routine. She appreciated the speed of the visits and knew she wouldn't feel like shit for the next week and a half. The laser simply felt like she was getting a sunburn every weekday. After three treatments, Whit was still able to spin gold out of straw with her positive outlook. "I'm continuously amazed at how detailed and precise the radiation process is. The setup for each zap takes far longer than the several seconds of the zap itself," she wrote on Caring Bridge. "It's too early yet to see/feel any improvements, but even as early as next week, things could start shrinking. I'm ready! One good part about radiation is there aren't the terrible side effects I've been managing. Mostly, things will feel increasingly sunburned, and there's more fatigue as the healthy cells work hard to repair themselves. I've never been a napper but am thoroughly enjoying an afternoon snooze with my fur-baby buddies!"

We got into a groove with the five-day-a-week radiation treatment routine, with Shirley and I taking turns driving Whitney back and forth to her brief appointments. During the week of Thanksgiving, the clinic closed Wednesday through Black Friday, so Whitney had a brief respite. I found this a bit odd, given that Hannibal, Dahmer, et al. didn't give a damn about holidays. We spent Turkey Day with Whit's family in Burnsville, where everyone gorged on turkey, gravy, stuffing and pumpkin pie, while Whitney rested, curled up on the couch. Not much giving of thanks on that day. The following Monday, we resumed the radiation treatments. By this time, Whitney had grown accustomed to being in a fair amount of pain, which she worked so diligently to alleviate with the palliative doc. But, on December 5, she entered a whole new dimension of discomfort. I was at a work conference in the western suburbs when I received her text. "So, when they lifted me up off the radiation table, I screamed because of my back," she wrote. "They've sent me to the ED to get the pain under control and probably do an X-ray to see if there's something wrong in there."

"Do you want me to come down there?" I texted back, looking for an excuse to flee the event. I could have been by her side at the hospital in under thirty minutes. The desire to eschew work and be with her was something I had wrestled with from the very beginning. Going to my job every day made me feel guilty on a couple of levels: a) for asking her mother to come up from Rosemount, a thirty-five-minute drive, so often, and b) I felt that I should be with my wife, who was in the battle of her life. Why the fuck was I at work?

"The ED doc is worried that I've got a tumor back there," Whitney responded. "Fucker! Mom's here… let's wait and see. We'll keep you posted!"

"For fuck's sake," I texted. "I was worried about that, too. Let's hope it's something else."

Three hours later, she texted an update: "Good news. I have arthritis! Haha (laughing emoji). Partly this flare-up is due to my inactivity… kind of limited on making that better, but I'll try. But no more tumors, so that's awesome."

"That is a big relief," I responded, then added: "Kind of perverse that having arthritis is something to celebrate."

"Right?!"

As my iPhone went to sleep, I thought to myself, "Arthritis? Really?" That didn't make any sense. She had metastatic breast cancer, and the ED doctor thinks the pain in her back is arthritic. I'm no physician but… I kept my skepticism to myself. I didn't believe it, but Whitney did, which provided her some relief, and that was good enough for me.

* * *

The next few weeks turned out to be our version of the movie *Groundhog Day*. We'd begin each morning with a shot of Lovenox, Shirley or I would drive Whitney in for her radiation treatment, then drive her back home, where she would rest for much of the day. I honestly don't recall what I was thinking at the time other than having a glimmer of hope still beating in my heart. It grew smaller, however, with each passing week, especially when I noticed the decline in her cognitive function. At first, I attributed it to the pain medication and the daily radiation doses. She could converse and communicate, but she wasn't the witty, sardonic woman I used to know.

On December 19, Lily flew in from Denver. Peter and Sam would join us over the next few days as we prepared to celebrate the holidays together. It went unsaid (as did so much in our cancer house), but it's likely we were all thinking the same thing—this could be our last Christmas together.

After Lily unpacked, the three of us went to a local restaurant for a soothing meal of ramen. Being the middle of December in Minneapolis, Whitney and her covered head did not stick out at the restaurant. For all the other patrons knew, she was just trying to stay warm, not hiding the fact that chemo had stolen her hair. We enjoyed a nice hot meal and shared a few laughs despite the awkwardness that hovered over the table. Whitney was not as sharp as usual. It was obvious. Lily tried not to let on, but I could tell she knew the light in her stepmother's eyes had faded.

Upon returning home, I reminded Whitney it was time for her nightly injection. She slowly climbed the stairs to our bedroom and waited for me to run through the usual procedure—I ripped open the packaging for the needle containing the medication, opened a bottle of isopropyl, moistened a cotton ball with the disinfectant, cleaned off the injection site on her belly, punctured her abdomen at an angle, pushed the plunger down, withdrew the needle, then pushed the plunger again until the protective shield clicked into place, rendering the needle harmless. I kissed her like usual, she thanked me and then I carried the spent needle down to the dining room where I kept a sharps container on top of our antique pie safe. As I climbed the stairs to finish the routine, which included putting the package of cotton balls and bottle of isopropyl away, I encountered Whitney on her way down, a frightened look on her face.

"What's the matter?" I asked.

"I drank some of the rubbing alcohol."

"What? You did what?"

"I thought it was my water bottle."

"How much? How much did you drink?" I started in hushed tones, not wanting Lily to hear.

"I don't know. Enough to know it wasn't water."

"Did you swallow it, or did you spit it out?" I asked, my voice rising.

"I don't know," she said, tearing up.

I tried to dial back my fear/anger. "That's poisonous, Whitney. Can we try to think of whether you just put it to your lips or actually swallowed it? It's important."

"I don't know. I didn't mean to do it." Embarrassed, she reverted to a little girl growing up in Apple Valley, fearing her father's reprimand.

I paused a moment and lowered my voice. "I know you didn't mean to do it, babe. But, if you drank a lot, it could hurt your stomach. We need to get it out of your system now." I guided her into the bathroom and shut the door. "I think you're going to have to make yourself throw up."

She shook her head. "I don't want to…"

"Do you want to go to the ER?" I asked, my voice rising again in anger despite my best efforts not to. "It's poison. We need to get it out of you."

"I don't want to throw up."

"And I don't want you to die."

She began to cry. Meanwhile, I bit back my anger. As calmly as I could muster, I said, "Just stick your finger down your throat, babe. It'll be over quickly, and then we don't have to worry." I did not want to take her to the hospital. The last time, before Halloween, she was there for nearly a week. If she went in now, how long would it be? A week? Two weeks? Longer? I know hospitals are there to care for people, to save lives, to cure, but at this point in her cancer fight, I saw them as yet another sign of a losing battle.

"Come on, babe. Can you do it for me?" She finally agreed to sit next to the toilet on the tile floor of our brand-new bathroom. Hearing the anger/fear in my voice, she reluctantly stuck a finger in her mouth and gagged slightly. Nothing came out. It scared her, though, and she refused to do it again. I pleaded. I begged. I knew that Lily was downstairs listening to this ridiculous argument, crying at the reality that her stepmother was dying, but Whitney wasn't going to throw up unless she wanted to. I couldn't force her. If she didn't want to do it, she wouldn't, so I gave up. She was already in bad enough shape battling the tumors. I didn't want to inflict further trauma.

We never figured out how much rubbing alcohol she consumed that night, but it didn't seem to have been enough to affect her gastrointestinal tract. We returned downstairs and sat in front of the television, not really watching whatever was on. Whitney stared blankly ahead. Lily wiped her nose and tried to hide her red eyes, while I replayed the last few moments over and over in my head. At this point, I was convinced that the cancer had spread to her brain. Was it simply a mistake—confusing a water bottle with an open container of rubbing alcohol—or was she not processing information properly anymore? My anger turned inward. Why hadn't I made sure that I had screwed the top back on the isopropyl? I should have been there for her. She needed round-the-clock care. What was I thinking? I had failed her.

* * *

Over the weekend, Peter drove up from Madison, Sam flew in from Pittsburgh, and all five of us tried our best to act like this would be a normal Christmas. We watched *Elf, The Christmas Story, Love Actually* and *The Holiday*, some of our annual favorites. We ate cookies, drank spiked egg nog, wrapped gifts and simply enjoyed each other's company. On Monday, it was back to reality and our regular radiation routine. I had taken the week off from work so I could take Whitney to her radiation appointment each day. On Tuesday, Christmas Eve, Whitney could barely function, shuffling along like a zombie. Her complete lack of energy made the doctors at the radiation center suspect that she had low blood cell counts, so they ordered a blood transfusion, just what everyone wishes for the day before Christmas. They checked her into Abbot Northwestern and got an IV into her to start the process. I settled back into a slightly padded vinyl chair next to her bed and tried to psych myself up for a day at the hospital. Instead, I sulked.

I had planned to make the family a big meal for Christmas Eve dinner featuring homemade lasagna, garlic bread, Caesar salad and a bottle or two of Zinfandel. Like troopers, Lily and Pete offered to don aprons and make the meal themselves. Given that lasagna is not an easy entrée for beginners, I figured they had no idea what they had volunteered for, but I appreciated that they were so willing to pitch in. By the time Whit and I returned home, it was after eight. We enjoyed the dinner Lily and Pete made, then opened a few presents before retiring for the night. The next morning Whitney woke up with a surprising amount of energy—the blood transfusion had worked.

Whitney put on jeans, a long cardigan, a T-shirt and a colorful knit cap. It was the most dressed up she had gotten in months. Pete and Lily put on some silly Christmas sweaters in an attempt to lighten the mood, then we drove down to Rosemount, where Grandma Shirley waited in her festive townhome, excited to host her children and "the grands." She had spent the days leading up to the event cooking all kinds of goodies—quiche, cheesy potatoes, and the kids' favorite, Monkey Bread, a sweet dough-y concoction that, if you are not familiar with, contains no monkeys. We spent the next few hours eating, drinking, opening presents and trying our best to ignore the elephant in the room. I don't recall any of the presents that year. The most cherished gift was being around family, having all the kids in town and seeing my wife's smile when we took what would turn out to be our last family photo.

Happy New Year, Hospital Staff

On December 29, after Lily and Peter had returned to Denver and Madison, respectively, Whitney woke up with a fever. We had no plans for the day other than to continue doing what we had been doing for the past several months—living with a cancer diagnosis and waiting for a miracle. Sam had made plans with Shirley to see *Little Women*, which they had been talking about for the past few days. A little outing would be good for them—to get away from the grief that had settled over our part of the world.

Whitney played the fever down at first, saying that it would go away. We knew that an infection would be bad and could lead to a return to Abbott Northwestern. Up until this time, despite being dealt bad card after bad card, I had held out hope that everything would work out. I normally describe myself as a realist, but in the case of Whitney's cancer, I wanted to be an optimist. The doctors knew what they were doing. They'd get her on the right program, and although it could take months, she'd get this illness under control, and eventually, our life would go back to normal.

Although I certainly didn't want her to end up in the hospital, I kept asking Whitney how she felt and suggested that to be on the safe side, we should probably go to the emergency room. By mid-afternoon, after Shirley had picked up Sam for the movie, Whitney said the fever was not abating and agreed to go in. I quickly compiled a go-bag of comfortable clothing and toiletries for her, got the dog secured in the basement and then escorted Whit out of the house into the cold December air.

I would like to think that we paused as we walked from the house to the garage to take in this moment but how were we to know that she would never return? That she'd never again see her bed, the brand new tiled bathroom, her refurbished claw foot tub, her Jacuzzi, her soap-making supplies, her Danish dining room table, her Nikon camera, her turquoise sectional, her orange mid-century modern chair, her spectacular braided dollar tree that had grown to within inches of the ceiling, her supply of Basil Hayden's, her homemade collection of bitters, her rock 'n roll T-shirt collection, her sporty red car, our cat Mr. Tom or Daisy the dog. No, we didn't pause to take one last look; we trudged forward with our ongoing battle against a foe we would not vanquish, not taking in the magnitude of any of our movements, not comprehending the significance of this overcast, bitter December day.

It was already dark when we arrived at the ER. I escorted Whitney to admitting and then was told where I could park so I didn't block traffic or get towed. When I returned, there was confusion, which I guess is nothing new. In the few times I've been in an emergency room, it's always been barely controlled chaos. As I've noted, Whitney's mind was shutting down. Plus, the gravity of the situation taking over and the fact that the attending doc didn't quite seem to have his shit together didn't help matters. I know emergency room physicians must assess situations quickly and that theirs is an extremely difficult job, but I've also seen them get many things wrong. On this day, the doctor fixated on her chemotherapy regimen, which, at the time, had been suspended for weeks. I corrected him twice, saying that she was in radiation, not in chemo. What the fuck? My wife is fucking dying here, doctor! Get your shit together. Am I stuttering? Am I not making sense? I'm pretty good at communicating. It's what I do for a living, for Christ's sake… After a few tense minutes, they finally checked her in and escorted us to a bay where they got her in a bed and began hooking up machines. They handed us masks and politely asked us to wear them. I secured mine and turned to Whitney to help her with hers, but she refused.

"Whit, you need to put the mask on," I said. "Doctor's orders."

"No."

"Why not?"

"Because I don't like them."

Given the gravity of the situation, I didn't want to fight with her, so I didn't persist. I thought of the episode ten days earlier when she drank the rubbing alcohol and refused to make herself vomit and suspected again that the cancer had affected her decision-making abilities. She just wasn't thinking right. The nurses and doctors continued to ask her to put the mask on, and she'd pull it off as soon as they left the bay.

"Babe, you should really keep the mask on," I whispered in her ear. "It's for your own good. This place is full of germs."

"I don't want to."

I stopped trying. Instead, I texted Sam and Shirley to tell them where we were. I figured it might take a while for them to get the message, assuming they wouldn't be checking their phones until after the movie ended.

Initially, the attending doc thought Whitney had pneumonia. I recalled the diagnosis just a few weeks earlier when the ER doc thought her intense pain when getting on and off the radiation board was due to arthritis. No, she didn't have pneumonia, I thought. It had to be the cancer. The answer was always the goddamn cancer. I kept it to myself, though, figuring they wouldn't want to hear my uneducated diagnosis. While we waited for a room in the hospital to become available, I heard from Sam and Shirley. They were headed to the hospital, their brief respite from reality coming to an abrupt end.

After an hour or so of waiting, a room opened in the hospital, and we transitioned from the ER to the third-floor oncology ward. Whitney's room had a view of a brick wall and was so small that you had to walk into the hall to change your mind. Whitney put on a hospital gown, and the nurses dropped off a pair of blue socks for her to wear. The blue color signified that she could move about on her own. Red meant you were a falling risk and needed to be escorted everywhere. She hated the concept of those damn red socks, seeing them as shackles that denied her freedom. Despite battling constant, growing, debilitating pain, she remained feisty. She loved the nurses and appreciated all that they did for her, but she hated whenever they helped her to the bathroom. Dignity is an early victim in a cancer fight.

* * *

With this hospitalization, we entered a new phase, one of expectation management. Whitney was no longer herself, the brave warrior taking on her fight with cancer with gusto. Instead, she shrank before my eyes, caving into herself, diminishing in weight, height, and now, cognitive ability. I put on a brave front, but that ray of hope inside me had dimmed considerably. When I drove home later that night, after Whitney had been officially admitted into the hospital and settled into a room, I soberly contemplated my life without her. She had been at this for four months, and along the entire way, we saw nothing but dark clouds. Time after time after time. I wanted to believe in miracles. In situations such as these, you must, but they don't come to everyone. Miracles aren't like trophies; everyone doesn't get one. They are rare; otherwise, they wouldn't be special. And, although God hears all our prayers, sometimes the deity says no. Resoundingly. I often wonder why Whitney got cancer, why this happened to her, to us, to her family, to me? And the answer is the same that we utter to our kids when they ask us to explain something that is either inexplicable or we're too tired to explain—because that's why.

When you lose a loved one, you can spend a lot of time blaming God. It's just a natural reaction to processing your grief. You blame him (or her or whatever) because he's taken your loved one away too soon. Whitney should have had at least twenty to twenty-five more years of life. Two more decades of watching our children grow and raise their own families, of traveling around the globe, of holding hands, of saying "I love you" excessively, of growing old together. It's easy to feel cheated, but we don't know the entire story. Perhaps when you die and have an audience with God, you'll spend the precious few minutes you get with him being a complete asshole complaining about what you lost or didn't get to experience rather than thanking him for your wonderful life.

"God, why did you take Whitney away from me so soon?" I might complain. "Women are supposed to live to be eighty in America. On average."

God would smile wistfully. "I know math is not your strong suit, Dan. But you know words, and you know what 'average' means."

At this point, I'd probably avert my eyes, perhaps stare at my feet, which would be either shoeless or adorned with sandals. This was Heaven, after all. My humility would dissolve quickly, and the asshole would return. "Yes, I know what average means. I'm just saying, fifty-four? She left the party way too early. We only had twelve years together. That's not fair."

God would have a good, hearty laugh at this, rattling Heaven's gates. "I'm going to let you in on something," he'd begin before launching into a lengthy explanation of why I didn't know what I was talking about. Nearby, St. Peter rolled his eyes.

"November 19, 2000, Whitney and Sam were traveling north on Highway 77 after celebrating Sam's fourth birthday at Shirley's house. Sam, strapped in solidly in the backseat, babbled away about everything and nothing, making her mother laugh as they drove home. Meanwhile, seventy-five-year-old Chester Olson was at the wheel of his 1980 Ford F-150 barreling south on 77. Chester had had a few too many at the Cedar Inn with his friends, celebrating a big Vikings' victory over the Panthers, and was now heading home to Lakeville with about half of his attention on the road and the other half focused on lighting another Pall Mall. Between lighting the cigarette, the nine Grain Belts in his system and the light rain now falling, it's a miracle he didn't lose control of his truck, cross the divided highway, plow into Whitney and Sam and kill everybody." God paused for dramatic effect as if talking with God wasn't dramatic enough. "Oh, wait, it wasn't a miracle that kept him from killing three people.

It was me. I kept him from losing control of the truck and killing your wife when she was thirty-five with four-year-old Sam in the backseat. I did that."

"That really happened?" I ask, because my brain sometimes resembles a misshapen rock.

"You doubt me?"

By now, a smarter man would have left with his tail between his legs.

"Here's another one for you, pal. When you say you were lucky to have met her, that's true. October 7, 1972. Leisure Lake. You and your brothers were hiking through the woods across the lake. Remember that? When you would take the jon boat over there and explore the woods looking for fossils and what not? On this day, you nearly walked right over a cliff. It was thirty-five feet to the forest floor below, a fall you might have survived if your head hadn't cracked open on a limestone boulder. You would have died almost instantly. You know why you didn't tumble over that cliff? Because I held you back from falling, the literal hand of me. So, don't waste any of your time whining to me, Dan. You and Whitney were lucky to have even met. You don't realize the pre-planning I do for some people. Fate schmate. I'm writing this giant book. Every damn day. Are you following me, son?"

"Yes, sir," I'd answer sheepishly, having been taken out to the woodshed by the Lord. "Appreciate the time we did have together?"

"Bingo." He winked. "Okay, I've gotta unleash a few tornadoes and display some rainbows. Peter will check you in and get you reunited with your wife."

So, I don't spend a lot of time blaming God. Blaming leads to bitterness, and bitterness should be left to coffee and alcohol. It's better to change your attitude. I am reminded of Viktor Frankl, the Holocaust survivor who wrote *Man's Search for Meaning*. He endured four years in a Nazi concentration camp in the most horrific, unspeakable conditions. He had plenty of reasons to be pissed off at his creator, to blame God for his suffering. And yet, he chose to remain positive, to adjust his attitude. "Everything can be taken from a man but one thing: the last of the human freedoms—to choose one's attitude in any given set of circumstances, to choose one's own way," he wrote, as well as this: "When we are no longer able to change a situation, we are challenged to change ourselves."

* * *

On New Year's Eve, a larger room with a nicer view became available across the hall at the hospital. They wheeled Whitney in, making a big deal about her new, luxurious space. "You can see the courtyard from here," the nurse said, as if Whitney planned to while away the hours gazing out at snow-covered Minneapolis. Although that was not on the agenda, Shirley, Whitney and I talked about how we could make the room homier with some fleece blankets and an essential oil diffuser, anything to mask that antiseptic smell of the hospital air.

I went home that night around ten thirty as the hospital lights softened and the regular turmoil of caretaking cancer patients diminished to the point of near tranquility. I sat down on the turquoise sectional in our living room with the cat on my lap and Daisy at my feet, turned on Cooper Anderson and Andy Cohen and started drinking. Whitney had been looking forward to 2020 and the upcoming election that held the promise that the current president would be voted out of office and the cloud of hate that had engulfed the country would dissipate with the winds of new leadership. Instead, I sat there alone to contemplate life without Whitney. The emptiness of our house and the stark reality of loneliness overwhelmed me. Was this how the rest of my life would play out? Pathetic and alone? Would I turn into Widower Hauser, the old man who yells at any kid dumb enough to walk across his property? Had I gone from the man who had everything and didn't realize it to the man who lost the love of his life and now had nothing?

The next morning Daisy woke me at six, and we went for a walk through the quiet, snow-covered neighborhood. We had escaped the shitty year that was 2019 and entered 2020 having absolutely no idea what lay ahead other than a continued battle with cancer, which seemed unwinnable. I ate a quick breakfast of oatmeal and secured Daisy in the basement, then made the ten-minute drive to the hospital. I had made the trip so many times it felt as if I could have done it in my sleep. I stopped in the café just off the main lobby and bought two cups of Starbuck's. The woman working the counter wished me a "Happy New Year," and I couldn't help but think, "what the fuck is *happy* about it?" I wished her the same and then took the stairs up another flight to the oncology ward. I entered Whitney's room with a smile and gave her a kiss on the forehead. "Good morning, babe," I whispered, setting her coffee down on the wheeled table, which was littered with a cup of ice water, the hospital menu, a box of tissues and some unused napkins. Whitney used to be a great lover of coffee, but by this time, she had no thirst, no appetite, no joie de vivre. She never touched the cup. Getting food into her system proved just as difficult. We'd order her something each day from food service, but it went uneaten. Whether it was the exhaustion of dealing with constant pain for the past four months, the depressing atmosphere of the hospital or simply Hannibal and his buddies eating away at her insides, Whitney seemed resigned to her fate.

Since Thanksgiving, she had not written any entries on her Caring Bridge page. A few days into the new year, I convinced her that we should give friends and family an update. For the first time, I wrote the entry, which we knew would communicate something completely different than her upbeat, humorous musings. It began with: "It's been a while. You're probably wondering, 'Where are the updates? What are Hannibal and Dahmer up to?' Quite a lot, unfortunately. Whitney's radiation treatments (five weeks' worth) have kept them at bay, but while the care team focused on those guys, others showed up—in her liver and her lungs." Normally, Whitney ended her entries on an up note, so I tried my best: "We truly appreciate everyone's support. We gain energy from your thoughts and prayers. So, keep up the good work! We are now asking you to turn up your prayers and good mojo a notch or two. Whitney continues to battle, but Hannibal and Dahmer, et al. are nasty mothers. They are not taking the hint that they are not at all welcome." I hit send, and the update went out to Whitney's family, friends and supporters. They provided tremendous support, positive salvos, and a lot of good energy. But would their words of encouragement do the trick?

* * *

For the past week, Dr. T had been out of the country on a family vacation. In her absence, we had dealt with a couple pinch-hitting physicians, who didn't seem to be reading Whitney's files as closely as I thought they should. I understand it's difficult to come in mid-treatment without having worked with a patient the entire way, but at the same time, you're dealing with someone's life, and it's your job to be on top of the care plan. You could spend a little more time getting some background before suggesting rote treatments. There, I said my piece. I don't blame any of her caretakers. She had great care; she just died. She could have had the best doctors in the world, and the outcome wouldn't have changed.

Upon her return, Dr. T suggested starting Whitney on Ibrance, a relatively new oral chemotherapy that is used in combination with letrozole, also designed to treat breast cancer in postmenopausal women. This combo would stop the cancer cells from growing, or so that was the hope. However, Whitney's insurance company would not approve these medications because they were not part of their formulary. Having worked for nearly ten years in the world of healthcare, I was quite familiar with prior authorization and the practice of denying certain medications because pharmacy benefit managers decided that they were too expensive. So, I understood the denial, but that didn't mean it would sit right with me. I'm not saying that if the insurance company had approved the medications Dr. T wanted to prescribe, they would have saved Whitney's life, but they might have, and the fact that the practice of prior authorization looked to be contributing to her string of bad luck just seemed like a slap in the face. If it weren't for bad luck, as the blues artists sing, she wouldn't have any luck at all.

The next few days, the healthcare team at Abbott focused on mitigating Whitney's pain. They wheeled in a patient-controlled analgesia (PCA) pump that allowed Whitney to self-administer morphine whenever she needed it. The device had a built-in timer, so once you hit the button, it wouldn't administer more morphine until a certain amount of time had elapsed. In her funk, she'd often forget when she hit the button and would try to get two doses of morphine in a row or would forget to depress it even if she had pain. More days passed, and nothing seemed to change except that Whitney moved around less and less. It became clear to Shirley and me, who were now at her bedside sixteen hours a day, that a white flag was slowly rising. There was no winning this battle.

On Sunday, January 12, two weeks after Whitney entered the hospital, Dr. T asked me to join her in the hall. I followed obediently with leaden feet. We passed various nurses and other hospital workers as they buzzed around, clicking info into computers, checking in on other patients, chatting about their Saturday nights. I steeled my nerves as I had a pretty good idea of what the doctor wanted to discuss. When we reached a less crowded area in the hall where we could talk privately, she turned and said somberly, "I'm sorry, but we're not making any progress here."

I nodded.

"Nothing is working. The chemo didn't work. The radiation didn't work. Insurance won't approve the Ibrance, and I'm not sure that would work anyway. Everything is so invasive at this point. Did you notice how happy she was when we told her she didn't have to do radiation anymore? It was just so painful for her to get up on that table. She was actually relieved."

I continued to nod, not quite sure what to say. I thought of the bell near the entrance of the radiation department downstairs, the one Whitney would not get to ring.

"Your kids are out of town, right?" she continued, not rushing but obviously not wanting to prolong the conversation.

A golf-ball-sized lump formed in my throat.

"I think you should get them here. I'm not saying it's going to be tomorrow or the next day, but the sooner they can get here, the better."

Usually not at a loss for words, I stood there completely stunned and mute.

"I've been doing this for over twenty years," she continued. "And this is one of the most aggressive cancers I've seen."

And so, there in the hallway on the third floor of the oncology wing of Abbott Northwestern, we decided Whitney's fate. I thanked Dr. T and told her that Whitney couldn't have had better care. "I appreciate that you didn't bullshit us, that you always treated us as adults and told us everything straight. I know that this must be the worst part of your job, and I don't know how you do it, but I want you to know that we appreciate it."

I returned to the room and shared my hallway conversation with Whitney and Shirley. Saying that we were done with the fight seemed like a script for someone else to speak. I couldn't believe the words were coming from my lips. The next step would be to call the kids and ask them to come home. Shirley excused herself from the room so that Whit and I could start with Sam. I won't share our conversation, only that it was excruciating. After we disconnected with the twenty-three-year-old, we sat silently, holding hands. Throughout the sickness, we did not dwell on the magnitude of what we faced. I know that Whitney was scared, but she didn't want to admit it. She wanted to appear strong so that I wouldn't get down. I did the same thing, and so like two stereotypical Minnesotans, we remained stoic, ignored the elephant in the room and missed the opportunity to share verbally our fear, anxiety, anger and remorse. We professed our love for each other but did not enunciate what life and death might be like without it. At the time, I felt it was the thing to do—put up a brave front. Now, I wish we had confronted it because ignoring it wasn't going to keep it away. I should have run toward the storm.

When Shirley returned from her walk, I'm sure she felt like she had entered a morgue. The ache of our call with Sam still lingered in the air. I excused myself and walked down to the Abbott lobby, where I called Lily and Peter to ask them to come home as soon as possible. Not much was said during the conversation; they seemed to know that the call was inevitable.

Just Follow the Ambulance, They Know the Way

It's a perverse experience to find yourself driving behind an ambulance and knowing that your dying wife is in it. But that's where I was on January 15, 2020, around 10:30 a.m., piloting my Rav-4 through the streets of south Minneapolis en route to a hospice in St. Paul. So many of the unknowns were becoming known. After eighteen days, we finally escaped the hospital. For the first week or two at Abbott, we wondered when we'd return home, then started to wonder if we would ever leave. Now, we were free but headed to a place where people go to die. It was a heart-wrenching conclusion, but we at least knew what lay ahead as opposed to frustrating and demoralizing uncertainty.

Dr. T had made it clear that Whitney was not responding to the treatments that she had prescribed. The cancer was winning, and a whole bunch of sugar-coating wasn't going to change that fact. Whitney accepted it, as did I and her mother. We simply had to decide how we wanted to write the final chapter—hospice at home or at a center. Shirley and I were prepared to follow Whitney's wishes. If she wanted to go home, we would rent a hospital bed, set it up in the main floor bedroom and make her as comfortable as possible. Hospice nurses would come in every day to tend to her needs, and a physician would stop by once a week to monitor her progress or lack thereof. Otherwise, the minute-by-minute care would fall upon two amateurs who loved her the most but knew nothing of palliative care. We'd be responsible for feeding her, bathing her and helping her climb a flight of stairs to the newly refurbished bathroom.

The other option would be to take Whitney to a hospice center where she would be made as comfortable as possible for her remaining days. She'd have round-the-clock care and a physician on staff who'd be available during daylight hours. Plus, there'd be a bathroom in her room. To Shirley and me, it was an obvious choice. Yet, Whitney longed to go home, see Daisy and Mr. Tom, and be around familiar settings. Shirley and I swallowed hard and assured her that it was her decision. The next morning on her second to last day in the hospital, Whitney changed her mind and said she wanted to go to the hospice center. Out of the blue. I was surprised. She seemed so intent on returning home and seeing the animals, her plants, her pictures, her new bathroom. We didn't question her decision, though. I could see the weight lifted from Shirley's shoulders. "That's for the best, Whitney," she said, kissing her eldest child's forehead. "They'll have everything there to make you more comfortable." Shirley looked at me and certainly could read the relief on my face, as well.

With Whitney's decision on where to go settled, the hospital staff reached out to the hospice to see if they had a room available. I immediately had a horrible, cynical thought—*If they don't have a bed now, they will soon.* No patient ever leaves a hospice on two feet. Everyone knows how the story is going to end, which made me think that working at a hospice must be one of the worst jobs ever. At a hospice, you tended to patients while juggling the mixed emotions of the family, whose attitudes wavered between complete disbelief to torrential sobbing. If you worked at a mortuary, at least you were dealing with certainty and family members were no longer filled with false hope. Yet, as I drove to the hospice for the first time behind the slow-moving ambulance, I felt perverse relief. Behind me, Shirley followed in her little red Versa.

We had told the kids to come to the hospice as soon as they got into town and started to communicate with friends that it was time to say goodbye. We were determined to fill the hospice with as much love for Whitney as we could.

The ambulance rolled up to the front door, and the EMTs had Whitney out on the stretcher going through the front door before Shirley and I parked our cars. Snow covered the parking lot, the roof of the red brick two-story building and everywhere else you could see in the quiet neighborhood. Cars buzzed by on the interstate just yards away. Although we couldn't see it because of the snow, to the side and back of the building sat beautiful landscaping and a peaceful yard.

Shirley and I crowded into the elevator with Whitney on her stretcher and the two EMTs. Fortunately, we only had to ride it for one floor because it was unbelievably slow and packed. The EMTs rolled Whit down the hall while the staff asked us to wait in the lounge so they could set up her room. For the next twenty minutes, few words were shared. I paced; Shirley stared off into the distance. The finality had sunk in. For however long it took, this would be Whitney's last residence. I had the urge to fill the silence but didn't know what to say. We could have expressed our sadness. We could have expressed our anger. We could have expressed our flagging faith in a higher power. How could God do this to us? Those with more faith than me would say it all happens for a reason; our job is to figure out why. How about it all happens for no reason? No reason at all? Perhaps, God made the Earth and the stars and then walked away, that everything that happens is pure serendipity, that he is nothing more than an omnipotent, absentee parent. This chaotic theory certainly made more sense to me than the idea that he controls everything, plays favorites, shows partiality to those who memorize the Bible.

I paused my pacing to take in the contents of the room. After all, we could be staying here for a while. Around us sat a variety of chairs, a recliner, several square tables, a long brown couch, a coffee machine, a flat-screen TV and all sorts of games and puzzles obviously to preoccupy people as they waited for their loved one to die. On the south side of the lounge was a glassed-in porch filled with a few chairs and some tables littered with more games and puzzles. I walked into the porch and realized it was too cold to spend much time in there during the winter. In the summer, it would have provided visitors with an open view of a courtyard filled with deciduous and coniferous trees, flowers, squirrels, rabbits, etc.

I rejoined Shirley in the lounge and the warmth.

"This is nice," she offered.

I nodded, knowing she meant the hospice center and not the horrific situation we reluctantly faced. "Yes, it is. Too bad I'm not much of a puzzle person."

"Not your cup of tea?"

"No, puzzles remind me of golf. You spend most of your time frustrated until you find a piece that fits. You feel a moment of elation and then return to complete frustration."

Shirley laughed.

I don't recall any more of the conversation, if there was any. We might have talked about how it would be nice to have all the kids home as if we were getting ready to celebrate Christmas again. I know we didn't talk about the things we should have discussed—like how damn scared we were.

Eventually, Jessie, an administrator from the center, asked us to come down to Whitney's room to start with the official check-in. We took a short walk down the hall and entered her room. Most of the other rooms on the floor housed two beds, but Whitney lucked out with a single. Whitney was in the bed, which had been placed in a sitting position. They had dressed her in a flowery smock that looked befitting of a ninety-year-old. We would get used to this clothing; I'm sure Whitney hated it but was too weak to protest. To her right, Whitney could view the tranquil tree-filled courtyard and the other annex of the center where the nuns resided. A pleasant view for an unpleasant stay. To her left, just a few feet away, a machine pumped oxygen into Whitney's nostrils. Beyond that, the bathroom.

For the next half-hour, Jessie reviewed the rules, regulations and schedules of the center and what to expect during Whitney's stay. Jessie finished her admissions spiel by pulling out a POLST form and began to explain it. I told her I was familiar. Her look back to me said sympathetically, "You've been through this before?" I explained that I worked in health care and knew that the form communicated to physicians a patient's life-sustaining wishes, whether to perform CPR and to what extent physicians should act to keep someone alive. I signed it and handed it back to her. Whitney and I had agreed long before she got sick that neither of us wanted to be kept alive at all costs and that we both wanted to be cremated. Because of my job, I felt that these were discussions that all couples should have.

Later that afternoon, the center's medical director stopped by and talked briefly with Whitney, Shirley and me before moving on to other patients. He made it clear that his top priority was Whitney's comfort. They'd be sure to get the right cocktail of medications and see that she felt as little pain as possible. Shirley and I appreciated his assurances. It made sense that their chief objective was to mitigate pain and suffering, given that the word "hospice" comes from the Latin word *hospitum*, meaning hospitality. The staff focuses on the patient's comfort physically and, often, spiritually. They are not there to prolong life but to provide solace and counsel to the patient and the patient's family.

Nuns were omnipresent, but Whitney did not call upon their services (though I'm sure the sisters prayed for her, just the same). When we checked in, Jessie made it clear that patients of all faiths (or no faith) were welcome. We were so grateful for the hospice team and how they made Whitney comfortable and provided the support the family needed. They didn't seem to mind when we took over the second-floor lounge, filling its refrigerator with leftovers from all the food guests brought when they stopped by to visit with Whitney and say goodbye. Nor did they seem to mind when we got a little loud, recalling funny stories about Whitney and her days in college and at work. The dichotomy of existence allows us to shed a tear one moment and laugh uproariously the next, to reflect upon the Earth's beauty and mankind's ugliness, to appreciate what we have and regret what we've lost.

Over the next week, a steady stream of those who loved Whitney visited. Like lottery winners, some were lucky to experience the quick-witted and salty personality

I had grown to love. Others were not so much and only witnessed the cancer-ravaged hollow shell struggling mightily to piece words together. Tears were shed. Hugs were exchanged. Questions to topics that just couldn't be reasoned away went unanswered. It didn't make sense. It wasn't fair. Life could be so cruel. Why? Why? Why?

Her long-time friend, Lisa, stopped by to perform some energy work. Jake and Laura visited and prayed over her. Abbie from Maryland and Becky from Colorado flew in from opposite sides of the country, both worrying that they would not make it in time to see her and then were relieved to find they had. Did they regret seeing her in her final form? Did they wish they could have preserved the image of a very much full-of-life Whitney walking around in their thoughts? Whitney didn't look like Whitney anymore. Bald head. Sunken eyes. Sharp cheekbones that looked like they might pop through her facial skin. Skeletal arms and shoulders. The life (and there had been so much of it) had been sucked out of her. I remembered how I felt as a twenty-one-year-old seeing my grandpa at the end of his life, ravished by cancer. He wasn't the same person I loved and admired as a boy, and it angered me.

* * *

The days at the hospice were filled with a soft din, food and reminiscing with family and friends. The nights, after family members went home to sleep in their own beds and try to replenish themselves for the next day, seemed to last forever as Sam and I took turns playing sentinel. Sam would begin the night shift sitting in the recliner in her mother's room, ready to assure her she was not alone if she woke in the middle of the night. I'd sleep on the couch in the lounge from 10:00 p.m. to 3:00 a.m. then we'd switch places. We were only getting three or four hours of sleep a night, and they weren't quality hours. Often, other families would come into the lounge and start up loud, anguished conversations. Because the lights were low, they wouldn't see me on the couch, and I ended up staring at the ceiling waiting for them to leave so that I could get some shut-eye. And if you were in Whit's room, you'd be awakened every few hours whenever a nurse or nun would come in to check on her. After several nights of this, Sam and I were completely spent.

By the end of the week, Whitney barely communicated. We felt she was hanging on simply because she was a headstrong, tough mother. Both Sam and I whispered into her ear that we loved her and that she didn't have to keep fighting, that she would be at peace and pain-free if she'd just let go. We continued looking for the ceiling people that the nurse had mentioned when we first arrived, but they refused to show. So, one day dissolved into the next. Family members were the only ones visiting now, bringing food, sharing stories and completing one puzzle after another. Upon check-in, we had been told that the average patient is there for fewer than three months, which in the grand scheme of life is just a blip on the radar. But, when you are operating on just hours of sleep and praying that your loved one is removed from the pain, it seems to last forever.

One of the nurses, who had been on the staff for several years, told Sam and me that patients will often hold on if their loved ones stay in the room constantly. "They don't want to die in front of you, especially their children," she said. "They will hold on sometimes just out of pride."

"So, you're saying it might move things along if we stayed away for a bit?" I asked.

"It might," she said. "You never know."

Sam and I discussed this at length—we didn't want her to die, but we didn't want her to continue suffering. We agreed that we needed a break from the constant vigil and decided to leave the hospice for dinner one night. Maybe that would give Whitney the opportunity to leave on her own terms. Imagine thinking that if you stopped your vigil for even just a couple hours, your loved one could die. As if we had that kind of power over life and death. At the same time, imagine being just outside the gates of Heaven with only pride keeping you out. That's the dilemma we faced.

By this time, I just wanted it all to be over. The pain, the suffering, the anguish, the misery, the waiting, the confusion, the guilt. I told the nurse on duty that we were going to slip away for some dinner, a break from the routine. She nodded knowingly. I felt like shit. I wasn't thinking like a good Christian—you don't give up hope, ever. You pray and you pray and you pray for a miracle, and then you pray some more.

We drove through a light dusting of snow to a nearby Irish pub, hoping that the hot food and cold drinks would get our minds off the task at hand, if only temporarily, and nourish us for the battle ahead. We ordered a round, then another and the alcohol entering our bloodstreams made us feel nearly normal. The feelings of guilt dissolved, and we began to smile and laugh because it's hard not to when you're in the confines of an Irish pub. Shepherd's pie, fish and chips, Irish stew filled the table and we stuffed ourselves. I didn't want to stop after two pints of Guinness because I knew one or two more would really get my mind off the situation back at the hospice, but I drove, and snow had covered the St. Paul streets.

We returned to the hospice two hours later, happy for the diversion but fearing what we had left behind.

Did Whitney take the opportunity to transition to the next dimension? Did she use the time alone to make her final exit? We entered the hospice, stomping our feet on the carpet in the vestibule, then climbed the stairs to the second floor. Most of our group stopped in the lounge to take off their coats and work on the latest puzzle, Sam and I continued onto Whitney's room, which we entered with great trepidation. A nurse was just leaving, shaking her head. We found Whitney lying there in a lucid state, the most alert she had been in a day or two, and she was not happy.

"She's trying to kill me," she said as we entered.

"What? Who is? Trying to kill you? What?" we stammered, confused to find her so agitated.

"That nurse tried to kill me. Where were you? Why weren't you here? She tried to kill me."

Sam sidled up to her bedside and took her hand. "It's okay, momma. It's okay. We went to dinner. We're here now." She stroked her mother's forehead.

My two-pint buzz immediately evaporated as I tried to figure out whether one of the nurses had actually hurt her unintentionally or was this the medications or just the cancer that had invaded her brain. "Are you talking about Nurse G?" I asked, referring to the nurse who had told us that some patients refuse to die in front of their loved ones.

Whitney nodded; her eyes filled with fear.

I kneeled on the opposite side of the bed from Sam and held Whitney's hand. "I'm sure she was just trying to help, babe."

"No, she was trying to kill me."

I kissed her forehead. "We're here now," I repeated in a soothing voice, cursing myself for agreeing to go to dinner. It was a stupid plan that had completely backfired.

Not only did she not pass on peacefully, but she suffered even more because of our absence. I stood up abruptly. Given my sour mood, I should have waited a few minutes before confronting Nurse G, but I needed to determine what had happened. I found her in the lounge talking with our group. I pulled her aside. "What happened in there? She says you tried to kill her."

Nurse G, who was nearly as tall as me and probably could have taken me in a back-alley scuffle, nodded her head with a sour expression on her face. "Yes, she grew rather agitated when we moved her and changed her bedding tonight."

"Was that necessary? Changing her bedding when she was obviously bothered by it."

"Standard operating procedure. We do that every night. I'm sure you've seen it before. You've been here long enough."

"Yes, I understand that, but when she's worked up, maybe you could have gone to some other rooms and come back later."

"Staff has a schedule it needs to maintain. I'm thinking that perhaps she was in an agitated state because none of her family was around." She let that float there for a few moments, then added, "I'm sure she has forgotten it by now."

I stepped back and looked over to Shirley and Whit's brother and sister who were doing their best to appear as though they had not been eavesdropping. I took a deep breath and decided to let it go. I excused myself and returned to Whit's room, where I found Sam scrolling through her phone, her mother asleep beside her. I quickly left the room and spent the next fifteen minutes walking off my anxiety in the halls of the hospice's two floors.

* * *

Except for sheer stubbornness, we couldn't understand what kept Whitney alive. She had always been an independent woman. She did not suffer fools easily, and behind closed doors, she'd let me know exactly what she thought of certain people. She was a strong woman who had endured and fought back against a lot of bullshit in her life from her failed relationships, to a strained relationship with her father, to being a survivor and then supporting other survivors. She mentored countless young female co-workers, knowing that they had a tougher road to travel simply because of their gender. The world needed more Whitneys, not fewer.

The last two nights—Thursday and Friday—Sam and I went home to sleep, partly out of sheer exhaustion but also because we thought it could be true that Whitney didn't want to let go in front of us, that she wanted to go on her own terms, alone. I remember the car ride being appropriately sedate. At home, we would have a drink, watch something goofy on Netflix and then retire for the night. I crawled into our queen-sized bed and lay there utterly drained and alone in its expansiveness, wondering what the next day would bring—more waiting or some finality to this chapter of our horror-story life.

* * *

The morning of Saturday, January 25, 2020, began like the previous nine days at the hospice, except Sam and I began it waking up at home rather than on the old couch in the hospice lounge or the recliner in Whitney's room. Although fitful, we both had gotten a full night's sleep, enough to face another day. We arrived at the hospice around 8:00 a.m.

and said good morning to a sleeping Whitney. The nurses said she had a peaceful night. I left Sam in Whit's room so she could take the first shift while I went to the lounge to get some coffee. Shirley showed up around 8:30 armed with treats for Shannon, who was celebrating her fifty-fourth birthday.

I remember sitting in the lounge's La-z-boy reading the Saturday paper. At some point, Sam came in to get some coffee, and Shirley told her she'd take the next shift. Sam looked depleted. My mother died in July 2017, so the memories of her passing were fresh in my mind. Yet, I couldn't imagine what Sam was going through. My mother was eighty-seven and died suddenly of a heart attack while snorkeling with her sister off the Galapagos Islands. A merciful, quick ending to a life well-lived. Sam, on the other hand, watched as her mother, still in the prime of her life, seemed to shrivel into nothingness before her eyes.

I went back to my paper, avoiding stories that featured the current president. My life was sad enough without being constantly reminded that America had elected a reality TV show host as its leader. A few feet away, Sam picked at the latest puzzle spread out on one of the lounge tables.

At around 9:15 a.m., Shirley entered the lounge and solemnly announced, "I think she's gone." Five months after first being diagnosed. Just under a month after leaving her home for the last time. Ten days into her hospice stay. Her battle was over. Her pain finally ceased. I didn't have the heart to ask Shirley if the ceiling people had visited. Raised a Catholic and well-attuned to the ways of God, Shirley would have let us know, I assume. The three of us walked down the hall and into Whitney's room, where a nurse confirmed Shirley's diagnosis. She went about her business quickly and then told us we could take as long as we wanted with her. "We'll move on to the next stage whenever you're ready," she said.

Whitney didn't look much different than she did when I had come in earlier in the morning to say hello and kiss her on the forehead. Except now, she was not breathing, her heart had stopped, her eyes remained closed. I kneeled between her bed and the window, which overlooked the snow-covered courtyard. Sam sat in a folding chair on the other side of the bed. Shirley stood at its foot. We had waited and prayed for this moment, but we had not fully prepared for it. I touched her hand tentatively, half expecting it to be cold. It wasn't. I held it and began crying like I had never cried before. I may have cried with such ferocity before, as a child, when a family cat had been run over by a car or I didn't get what I wanted for Christmas, but never for such length. A child's sadness passes like a summer storm; mine lingered like a March snowfall producing such volume that you begin to wonder if it would ever stop. Across from me, Sam's shirt and sweatpants grew splotchy as they absorbed her tears. Her mother, my wife, Shirley's oldest, had left the party early.

Epilogue

Why hadn't she come to visit? Months had passed. I had hoped, prayed and bargained but still saw no sign of her, either as a ghost or in my dreams. Please come to me, Whitney, I pleaded. Show me there's an afterlife, that we will meet again.

Instead, she visited someone else. "She came to me in a dream," Lisa, the spiritual advisor/energy healer, told me in an email on what would have been Whitney's fifty-fifth birthday, two and half months after she passed. "She said she was fine, that she was free of pain and at peace. So, don't worry," she wrote. I thanked her, went into the living room, curled up into a ball, and sobbed for half an hour. Why Lisa? Why hadn't she come to me? Her husband? The love of her life? What about my pain? Didn't I need assurance that she was okay?

* * *

A few weeks later, I woke up abruptly in the night. I looked at my watch. Three fifteen. The time when shit always happened in *The Amityville Horror*. It's the scariest time of the night, right? Dark. Quiet. The city is asleep. No sirens. No barking dogs. Too early to get up. Too late to be awake. Biorhythms say, "You shouldn't be doing anything but sawing logs." Doubt me? Try walking in a straight line when you're dead tired. It's like you're drunk. And yet there I lay, eyes wide open. Unable to fall back asleep. I had learned long ago never to trust anything my brain said between 1:00 and 4:00 a.m. It made up all sorts of crazy shit. Once, it told me to go back to my first wife using the argument that it would be a lot easier to just put up with her idiosyncrasies than to start over and try to find love again. Back in college, it had tried to convince me that life wasn't worth living, even though I was at the height of my vim and vigor when I normally felt indestructible. My late-night brain's most egregious suggestion came the night my daughter was born, some nine hours after she took her first breath—it told me to kill her. I knew my brain was exhausted and really should be excused for suggesting such evil shit, but it pissed me off, nonetheless.

If there was a time of day in which Whitney could appear as a specter or simply as a vivid figment of my imagination, it would be at 3:15 a.m. I didn't care what form she took. I just wanted to see her in something more than just picture form. Three-dimensional would be great even if I could see right through her. And if she could speak, that would be even better. I once called her phone just to hear her voice, but it was just the automated woman's voice reciting her phone number. Leave a message, the stranger told me. I wish I had captured her on video, even a snippet on my iPhone. I was forgetting how she sounded. How she laughed. How she cleared her throat. How she sighed. How she yawned. How she sneezed. How she blew her nose incessantly between the months of November and March. How she hiccupped and hiccupped and hiccupped. She hiccupped a lot, more than anyone I have ever met. She went through jars of peanut butter (her cure for ending hiccup outbreaks) faster than Reese's.

But she never appeared.

* * *

I hate the thought that I will *never* see her again. Never. Again. It makes me angry. I don't want to believe it, though the rational side of me, which is pretty much four-fifths of me, knows it to be true. That's the dichotomy of my existence. Rational vs. emotional. Thinking vs. feeling. As I get older, I am trying like hell to *feel* more, like Whitney. She was smarter than hell, and often she just let things develop without overanalyzing everything. She felt things. I know it's not right to make her out to be a saint. She wasn't. But, in death, she becomes more divine with each passing day.

The tendency, at least in the first few months after her death, was to conjure up the grisly images of her last few months on Earth. The early meetings with Dr. T as she diplomatically told us what could happen next, meetings in which I could not regulate my body temperature, meetings in which I always felt on the verge of passing out or simply fleeing just to get away from the bad news. Then the chemo sessions, which I hope I never have to endure. I don't know that I would even be able to. Then the radiation treatments, which seemed more bearable than the chemo but not necessarily less invasive. It's all horrific and hard to believe that Whitney had to go through it, and I was witness to it all.

* * *

The first time I got laid off from a job, I went six months without steady work. And although I had no trouble getting interviews, no offers came my way. It seemed like I was always the second choice. Someone always turned out to be a little better or smarter or had more charm than me. I began to worry that I would "never" get a full-time job again. And then I did. After my divorce, I went out on date after date after date. Some went okay, others were complete dumpster fires. Nothing seemed to click. On my more pathetic, self-loathing days, I'd lament, "I'll never fall in love again." And then I did. Never say never, they say. But when you are dealing with death, and you are a rational, thinking being, and you have absolutely no evidence to the contrary, death is the end. It is the last out in the bottom of the ninth. The period at the end of a sentence. Yes, she lives on in my memory and in the heads of everyone who knew her, but we will never again go out for burgers and drinks at our favorite pub. We will never cheer on the Loons at Allianz Field, or, more accurately, I will never sit next to her and cheer on the Loons while she scrolls through her smartphone, checking all her social media accounts.

* * *

Because of Whitney, I fear death a lot less than I used to. If there is a Heaven, I have someone waiting for me. We will be reunited, and it will be wonderful. I hope she will be proud of me, how I lasted and endured during her absence. Maybe in Heaven, time doesn't really exist. Maybe to her, it won't seem like an eternity since we last held hands, or said, "I love you," or sat on the couch all Friday night long watching episodes of *Criminal Minds* or *Diners, Drive-ins and Dives*. I hope she tells me I did the most with my time alone, that I didn't let the grief consume me and render me into a useless pool of tears. I'll start to tell her about what she missed, and she'll pat my arm and say, "I was with you every step of the way." And then, I'll look at her concerned and ask: "Every step of the way? Even when I, you know…" She'll laugh and say, "You would go there, wouldn't you? No, I didn't watch everything you did. The living deserves some privacy." This would come as a huge relief because, for a while, I watched a lot of porn on lonely nights.

* * *

Three years have passed since I lost the love of my life. I don't know which steps to take next. According to US actuarial tables, I will live for twenty-four more years. That's a long time to live alone although I've grown accustomed to a silent house. I don't have to ask anyone what they want for dinner or which tv shows to watch. But then I think, was it what we were watching or was it that we were watching it together?

A friend of mine questions whether I should go around saying that Whitney was the love of my life. "Who wants to compete with that? You're going to scare women off saying such things," she says. She does have a point; it does sound intimidating. I've met several widows/widowers who say they have no intention of ever dating again because they don't believe they'll ever find someone as special. I refuse to believe that, though. My heart, I believe, is of infinite size. Parents who have one child don't avoid having another because they wonder if they could love the second as much as the first. The heart expands to allow for that additional love. At least, that's what I'm counting on. And yet, dating scares the shit out of me.

I remember the craziness of dating after my divorce, and although Whitney and I met online, it's hard to imagine lightning striking again. Am I just wasting my time? Will it just be one frustration after another, bearing no fruit?

I certainly felt that way at times after my divorce and re-entry into the dating scene. The odds may be stacked against me, but I won't let fear of loss or rejection keep me from that ultimate prize—romantic love. I miss sitting across the table from someone at dinner. I miss staring into someone's eyes. I miss splitting a bottle of wine. I miss sharing a laugh. I miss someone rubbing my back and telling me everything is going to be okay. I miss hugging. I miss kissing. I miss necking. I miss undressing someone. I miss exploring someone's body. I miss the feeling of skin on skin. I miss being inside someone when two become one. I miss falling asleep holding hands. I miss being a couple. I miss joy. I miss being complete.

* * *

Before I go, I'll leave you with this. It's neither new nor unique, but it's born out of the ashes of a tragic love story.

>Love with all your heart.
>Take chances.
>Don't waste time.
>Tell people how you feel about them regularly.
>Stay positive, even when the bullshit is piled high.
>Be kind to others, even if they aren't to you.
>Volunteer your time and help those less fortunate.
>Get out and enjoy nature.

Finally, and I borrow this from musician Warren Zevon, who died of cancer too young, *enjoy every sandwich*. Now it's on to my third act.

Acknowledgements

Although I walk the path solo, I am not alone. Knowing that there are others carrying similar burdens provides me with peace of mind.

First and foremost, I want to thank my family. For helping me remember what I had chosen to forget. For proofing early versions of the book. For propping me up when I was down. Thank you, Lily, Peter, Sam, Shirley, Shannon, Jason, Steve, Mary, Matt and Mike.

Thank you to Joe and Linda, good, good friends who have often carried me when I was too tired to walk.

Thank you to my fellow widows and widowers at the hospice grief group. May your days be filled with peace and love. To helpful friends from my past who have also lost a spouse too soon. We find solace and comfort in each other's stories. We are all members of a club for which no one wants to belong.

Thank you to my therapist for helping me navigate my grief and keep it in place.

Thank you to Calumet Editions for their guidance and professionalism. To Beth Williams, the sharpest of editing eyes, Gary Lindberg, who developed this arresting cover, and Ian Graham Leask, who first suggested I turn the novel I had been planning to write on Whitney's passing into a memoir. Wise counsel, my friend.

Thank you to all of those of you who have chosen healthcare as a profession, especially to the staffs at Abbott Northwestern Hospital, Minnesota Oncology, and the Virginia Piper Cancer Institute. You are amazing at what you do.

And thank you to all of my friends, neighbors, co-workers and co-volunteers who picked me up when I fell. We don't get through this life alone. Know that I have your back, too. Peace.

About the Author

Daniel Hauser is a creative writer based in Minneapolis. He has written for a variety of local, national and international publications during his 25+ year writing career. He is originally from Davenport, Iowa.

www.ingramcontent.com/pod-product-compliance
Lightning Source LLC
Chambersburg PA
CBHW031956080426
42735CB00007B/410